What would Marx do?

What would Marx do?

How the greatest **political theorists** would solve your everyday problems

Gareth Southwell

FIREFLY BOOKS

A FIREFLY BOOK

Published by Firefly Books Ltd. 2018

Design and layout copyright © 2018 Octopus Publishing Group
Text Copyright © 2018 Gareth Southwell
Cover art and caricatures on pages 7, 8, 19, 41, 44, 47, 64, 80, 93, 105, 116,
130, 150 and 159 © 2018 Gareth Southwell Illustration
All other illustrations © 2018 Grace Helmer

First printing

Publisher Cataloging-in-Publication Data (U.S.)

Library of Congress Control Number: 2017953715

Library and Archives Canada Cataloguing in Publication

Southwell, Gareth, author
    What would Marx do? : how the greatest political theorists would
solve your everyday problems / Gareth Southwell.
Includes bibliographical references and index.
ISBN 978-0-228-10030-0 (softcover)
    1. Conduct of life--Miscellanea. 2. Political science--Philosophy--
Miscellanea. 3. Philosophy--Miscellanea. 4. Ethical problems--
Miscellanea. I. Title.
BJ1589.S68 2017   170'.44   C2017-905883-5

Published in the United States by
Firefly Books (U.S.) Inc.
P.O. Box 1338, Ellicott Station
Buffalo, New York 14205

Published in Canada by
Firefly Books Ltd.
50 Staples Avenue, Unit 1
Richmond Hill, Ontario L4B 0A7

Printed and bound in China

First published in Great Britain by Cassell,
a division of Octopus Publishing Group Ltd
Carmelite House
50 Victoria Embankment
London EC4Y 0DZ
Gareth Southwell asserts his moral right to
be identified as the author of this work.

Editorial Director: Trevor Davies
Junior Editor: Ella Parsons
Copyeditor: Robert Tuesley Anderson
Art Director: Yasia Williams
Designer: Ella McLean
Production Controller: Sarah Kulasek-Boyd

Contents

Introduction

It feels as if the world is becoming more political. Or maybe it's just that, through social media and the internet, we are all now more exposed to political issues. If we want to, we can now find news updates 24 hours a day, on almost any topic and from anywhere on the planet. So, whether it's the growing threat to Southeast Asia's coral reefs, the heart-rending plight of Syrian refugees, the extravagant excesses of Wall Street traders, or some more local issue, it's now much easier to stay informed, get involved, share and comment, promote or condemn. This also makes it much harder to escape from it all, as – perhaps more so than ever – we are exposed to the political opinions of friends and casual acquaintances, work colleagues and even complete strangers.

Of course, it's not just in reading or discussion, online or in the media, that we are faced with political issues, but also, as we go about our daily lives, in the form of common practical dilemmas. Should you buy fair-trade coffee? Do you have a moral duty to give to charity? Is there any good reason to get married, and is it a good idea to have children? Is it OK to want a better job or a bigger house? Even whether you should wear a bicycle helmet, or look after a friend's pet. These might not seem like political questions at first, but, when you look deep enough and in the right way, you will find that political philosophers have had lots to say about such questions. So, Plato might not have explicitly addressed the question of Facebook-addiction, but he had lots to say on the role of government in helping us to be rational and free from destructive passions. John Stuart Mill never saw a tweet in his life, but would have argued that your right to say what you want on social media should be limited as little as possible. Therefore, when we ask "what would Marx do?", and consider how the great political minds would have dealt with everyday situations in the 21st century, it is not some frivolous exercise, but a serious attempt to understand how the insights of some of history's great political thinkers might be applied to our everyday lives – which, after all, is what politics is about, isn't it? How we live our lives?

Underlying most common dilemmas that we face are various unquestioned assumptions: ethical attitudes about the nature of good and duty; beliefs about the freedom and power of the individual in relation to the state; views concerning justice and fairness; or regarding the

distribution of wealth and poverty; and so on. In analysing these mundane problems, we can therefore unearth and explore these issues, and find out what a wide spectrum of political philosophers have had to say about them. As you might expect, they didn't always agree, and so in considering their different views you will not always end up with a simple piece of advice that you can follow and apply – that's not really the point of philosophy. Rather, what you'll get is a deeper understanding of *why* the issue in question has been so contentious,

and why many of them continue to be the subject of vigorous disagreement. By the end of it, you'll know what Marx would have done, and Plato, and Mill, and Aristotle and Hegel, and many others besides. Some you'll agree with, and others you won't, and you'll probably be left with many more questions than you had before – but that's just the nature of philosophy. However, with that understanding, you'll also be in a better position to make up your own mind, and to answer the most important question: "What would *I* do?"

Freedom

Chapter 1

My car has just been stolen! But can I hold the thieves responsible?

Democritus • Sartre • Hobbes

At first, you think you've just forgotten where you parked. Then, gradually, with a mixture of horror and disbelief, it dawns on you: your car has been stolen. Maybe it's your own fault. You shouldn't have parked the car down that shady side-street. And this isn't exactly the best neighbourhood. And the car itself – I mean, a Bugatti Veyron EB 16.4 is almost *asking* to be stolen.

Later, the police contact you. Your car has been found burned-out, and the culprits have been caught – some local teenage delinquents on a joyride. "Don't worry," says the police officer, "they'll get what they deserve." But should they?

At the root of all questions of political freedom – or "liberty", as it's often termed – is the deeper question of to what extent we have *free will*. Most political philosophers assume that we have it, to some degree. After all, how can you vote if you don't really have a say in what you decide? How can you be held accountable for your actions if you are not ultimately in control of them? To ask whether we have *liberty*, we must first assume that we have *free will*. But do we?

Determinists and indeterminists

Ever since the Greek philosopher **Democritus** (*c.*460–*c.*370 BCE) first proposed that everything that exists consists of atoms, the idea that everything that happens might be down to nature – not God or "fate" – began to take root. As science developed, identifying the laws that govern matter, a *materialist* conception of

human beings became possible, one where soul or spirit played no part. However, if we are merely atoms, and the behaviour of those atoms necessarily obeys physical laws, does that mean that our actions, too, are determined by those laws? But doesn't that mean that we're *not* free? That life is just a meaningless piece of theatre? And what does that mean for political freedom?

The belief that we have no real freedom of the will is known as *hard determinism,* but there are also various *soft* varieties.

I am a victim of circumstance!

My existence precedes my essence!

10

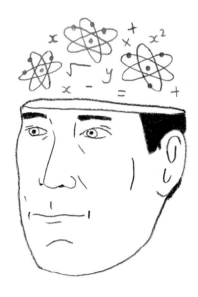

For instance, we may argue that our early experiences in life shape who we are, as do economic factors (how well-off our family was), the attitudes and expectations of our parents and friends, as well as our educational experiences. Such *environmental* factors may therefore partly determine our actions in life. This doesn't mean that we have no ultimate freedom to choose, but merely that not everything about what we are and do may be freely chosen, and that behaving morally and rationally may be harder for some than for others. One defence of your teenage joyriders may therefore be that they've grown up on the "wrong side of the tracks"; that, given a better start in life, they would not have become delinquent at all. Before we talk about liberty and accountability, shouldn't we therefore also consider social and environmental factors? Even, perhaps, the possibility of the influence of "bad genes"? Of course, *genetic determinism* can also be "hard" or "soft": perhaps *everything* we do is hard-wired or maybe, like other factors, genes provide only a tendency, an influence that can be overcome.

If determinism broadly argues that we have no real freedom (or, at least, less than we think), then the opposite view – *indeterminism* – argues that our choices are freely made. (Such a view is also sometimes called *libertarianism*, which confusingly is also the name of a political philosophy – *see* page 89.) As already noted, this standpoint is important for many political doctrines, which generally assume us to be responsible for our actions. As there are hard determinists, so there are hard indeterminists. For instance, French existentialist philosopher **Jean-Paul Sartre** (1905–80) argued that "Existence precedes essence", by which he meant that what we are (our "essence") is not determined by human nature, or genetics, or any outside factors, but must be something that we choose *after* we are brought into existence. As such, it is our choices that define us, nothing else: "In life, a man commits himself, draws his own portrait, and there is nothing but that portrait." Returning to your car thieves, Sartre would argue that they were responsible for their choices, no matter what other mitigating circumstances there were – they cannot blame their background. Sartre's notion of freedom is therefore *radical*; even in prison or at gunpoint, you are still "free", because you may still choose how you respond to those situations. Freedom does not therefore mean complete control – getting whatever you want – but rather freedom to *think* and *act* how we want. Even if there seem to be limits upon our actions, we still have freedom of choice (even if we don't like the consequences).

Sartre himself was very politically active, so we should not assume that he did not care about political freedom. In terms of political liberty, however, radical freedom would seem as problematic as hard determinism. Aside from the question of whether I do actually possess free will, if we are free *no matter what* our circumstances, then how does that help us decide (for instance) how much power the state should have over us, or what I am legitimately allowed to do in society?

The middle ground – compatibilism

Arguably, a more politically useful definition of freedom can be arrived at if we adopt a middle ground. Such a view is known as *compatibilism*, as it argues that a person may be said to possess a degree of freedom (he or she may make choices and be accountable for them), while also leaving open the possibility that there are mitigating factors beyond his or her control (environmental, social or even genetic factors). A compatibilist will therefore argue that, while, in a sense, all things are determined by cause and effect, we may be said to be free in as much as our actions are based on our own motivations.

> ## Basic philosophical question:
> What is the nature of political freedom? How does it relate to the deeper question of freedom of the will?

A well-known compatibilist is the English philosopher **Thomas Hobbes** (1588–1679). In his book of political philosophy *Leviathan* (1651), he characterized freedom as "absence of opposition". In other words, if you want to do something, you can do it, and no one is stopping you, and it can be said that you are "free" to do it. Political freedom is therefore simply freedom from external coercion, where the individual may follow his or her reasonable desires within legal limits. Of course, the law itself is a form of external restraint: laws stop you doing things, and, if you break them, the state would be entitled to *coerce* you to obey – by physical force or, by taking away some of your freedoms, through physical imprisonment. The extent

> *"[T]he liberty of the man…consisteth in this, that he finds no stop in doing what he has the will, desire, or inclination to do."*
> Thomas Hobbes

to which you are free is therefore also determined by the extent of the law and the power of the state. So, Hobbes thought, as long as you obeyed the law, then there was a sphere of life that was just yours, within which you could be free.

It seems fair to say that the state should regulate at least some of our social behaviour – after all, our actions may affect others, curtailing their own freedom. The car thieves' desperate desire to drive my Bugatti Veyron EB 16.4 conflicts with my desire to retain ownership of that car; therefore, the state should protect my right of ownership against their illegitimate desire to steal it. In terms of their accountability, no one was forcing them to steal it (as far as we know), and, since we may argue that they were therefore free *not* to steal, we must hold them accountable for their actions.

And the debate goes on...

But what about soft determinism? What about all those genetic influences, the social deprivation, the turbulent home lives, all of which may have contributed to the thieves' criminal behaviour? Shouldn't they be judged more leniently? Doesn't the state have a duty to work to alter those determining factors?

The free will versus determinism debate is a very old and complex one, and still rumbles on, and we may say that there's still no complete agreement on the matter. Also, as you can see, while it's a separate issue, it does have relevance to the question of political liberty. For even if we admit that we all possess free will, there is still the question of whether all of us possess it equally, and what part external factors play.

Making a decision:

While we may like to think of questions of law and criminality in black-and-white terms, a closer look reveals that it may not be so simple. Your car thieves, while they may possess "free will" in Hobbes's sense, are also the products of social, biological and environmental forces. So, while we might like to agree with Sartre that we all equally possess "radical freedom", a more justifiable and compassionate perspective will allow for the possibility that there may be other factors that shape and influence the thieves' decisions. And, if we were to swap our backgrounds for theirs, do we know for certain that we would behave any differently?

My friend says that I'm getting too fat. But, surely, it's none of her business?

Hobbes • Machiavelli • Plato • Mill

Some friendships are robust, encouraging mutual honesty and openness, and seem able to withstand anything; others are more fragile, awaiting only a single thoughtless remark to bring them crashing down. So, from that point of view, it all depends on which type your particular friendship takes, and where you both agree "the line" is. However, the question of how your actions affect others, and at what point others may have a right to intervene, is a central one in political philosophy. The main issue here is the potential conflict between individual freedom and the rights of others not to be affected by your actions.

Order, order

In answering this question, many philosophers have favoured order over freedom. **Thomas Hobbes** took such a dim view of human nature that he thought that this justified an all-powerful state, with sweeping, pervasive powers. For Hobbes, maintaining social order was of such importance that the state might be justified in almost any degree of intervention. Similarly, the Italian political philosopher **Niccolò Machiavelli** (1469–1527) advocated all manner of oppression and underhand dealing in order to maintain authority. In *The Prince* (1532), a sort of textbook for would-be rulers, although he admitted that "the best possible fortress is – not to be hated by the people", a ruler cannot always count on being popular. Faced with a choice, he therefore argued, "it is much safer to be feared than loved". Even the ideal republic imagined by the Greek philosopher **Plato** (*c.*429–347 BCE) was not one of individual freedom, but rather a carefully structured hierarchy, where only the most "rational" were fit to rule and everyone else was allotted a place according to birth and educational merit.

Classical liberalism – the individual as sovereign

It is only really in the 19th century, with the development of what is known as *classical liberalism*, that political philosophy begins to emphasize the rights of the individual. One of the key developments of classical liberalism was its emphasis on *civil liberties*, or those personal freedoms of the individual that the power of the state cannot curtail. One of the most famous expressions of this view can be found in *On Liberty* (1859), a work by the English utilitarian philosopher **John Stuart Mill** (1806–73). Mill was especially concerned with what he termed the "tyranny of the majority" – that is, the power of the majority within a democratic

14

state to suppress the views and interests of those who are in a minority. As an illustration of Mill's point, we can see how, if most people within a democratic state were Catholic, its laws and customs would reflect that – laws on marriage and divorce, on contraception and scientific research, for example. Since most elected officials and politicians within such a state would be drawn from the majority view, and public opinion and pressure groups would try to influence the government to adopt certain laws that are in the majority's favour, then it's difficult to see how the minority, and the rights of the individual in general, might be protected. Mill proposed that the only way to ensure personal freedom was to limit the power of the state, so that all individuals, no matter what their beliefs, are allowed freedom to act, speak and think exactly as they please, *provided there is no harm to others.*

This view, which has since become known as Mill's principle of harm, is a radical defence of personal freedom. For Mill, the only reason that the state can force an individual to do (or not do) something is to protect other members of society. And so, "The only part of the conduct of anyone, for which he is amenable to society, is that which concerns others. In the part which

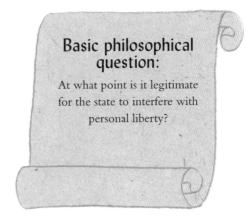

Basic philosophical question:
At what point is it legitimate for the state to interfere with personal liberty?

merely concerns himself, his independence is, of right, absolute. Over himself, over his own body and mind, the individual is sovereign."

So, just to be clear, here: the "harm" in question is only in relation to others; if the action is "self-regarding" (as Mill termed it), no matter how harmful that person's actions, the state may still not intervene. Want to stay at home all day and eat cream cakes until you die of coronary disease? Fine! Spend every night passed out in an alcoholic stupor? Go ahead! Your friend may, of course, express her disapproval – she would rather not see you eat or drink yourself to death, so she might try to persuade you to stop your excessive behaviour or seek professional help. But the only basis on which the state can legitimately

"*The only purpose for which power can be rightfully exercised over any member of a civilized community, against his will, is to prevent harm to others.*"
John Stuart Mill

Mill's Principle of Harm

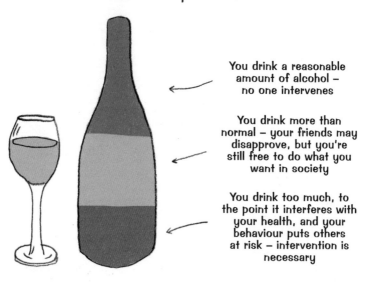

You drink a reasonable
amount of alcohol –
no one intervenes

You drink more than
normal – your friends may
disapprove, but you're
still free to do what you
want in society

You drink too much, to
the point it interferes with
your health, and your
behaviour puts others
at risk – intervention is
necessary

intervene is if the actions in question cause harm to another person. A man who is an alcoholic may find it difficult to hold down a job as a bus driver, may become short-tempered or forgetful, and so on, but it is only at the point at which the person's alcoholism causes him to neglect his duties – by causing a traffic accident, by being drunk at work – that his condition becomes a public concern.

The limits of personal freedom

But what if, instead of "slow death by cream cakes", you planned to commit suicide? Mill never explicitly discusses this question, but he does raise a related point. If you signed some horrible contract that essentially made you your employer's slave, then the state could intervene to free you from it, despite your having freely agreed

> *"The best friend is he that, when he wishes a person's good, wishes it for that person's own sake."*
> Aristotle

> *"Whatever crushes individuality is despotism, by whatever name it may be called, and whether it professes to be enforcing the will of God or the injunctions of men."*
> John Stuart Mill

to its terms. As Mill says, "The principle of freedom cannot require that [an individual] should be free not to be free." Our reason for *not* interfering in another's self-harming acts is to protect that person's liberty; but, in relation to suicide, if you're dead, there's no liberty to protect! To protect someone's liberty, then, the state may prevent you killing yourself, for – though it may sound odd – it would be ensuring your liberty!

But, even if we accept this application of Mill's principle, what's the difference between habitual self-harm (killing oneself slowly) and suicide (killing oneself quickly)? And on what grounds could your friend interfere in the latter but not the former? This is a question that is still debated, especially in terms of "assisted suicide", but the bottom line – and one reason why Mill might have resisted advocating intervention in suicide – is that such interference would be a *slippery slope*: intention to commit suicide is a definite act, but since how we define "harm" is to an extent subjective, your friend might start with saving you from your intended death, then "death by cream cakes", and finally end up forbidding cream cakes altogether – and what a world *that* would be!

Making a decision:

The question of whether your friend is "allowed" to make personal comments is really down to the sort of friendship you have. However, it opens up the broader question of whether individuals are free to live their lives as they wish, and when the state may intervene. Hobbes, Machiavelli and Plato all favoured preservation of order over individual freedom, while Mill argued that, to protect liberty, we must confine the power of the state almost solely to those actions that affect others. Your weight and cream cake consumption are issues for the state only insofar as they affect your public duties. Your friend can say what she likes – if she is still your friend...

Should I watch what I say on Twitter?

Mill • Feinberg • Greenwald

You're trending again. You didn't mean to, but your humorous meme poking fun at a religious cult has gone viral, and now the secretive cult's high-powered lawyers are threatening you with all sorts of legal nastiness. But it's a free country, right? Can't you say what you want?

Freedom of speech has long been enshrined as a fundamental principle of democratic society. The First Amendment to the US Constitution guarantees it, and the *Universal Declaration of Human Rights* (1948) broadens this out into "freedom of expression", thus covering both spoken and written communication, whatever the medium. However, as with action, free expression is generally thought to require limits so as to protect the public.

John Stuart Mill's *On Liberty* (1859) allots a great deal of space to defending the value of free speech. In a democratic society, those in power, representing the majority, are often tempted to suppress what they consider extreme, immoral or harmful views, or simply views they disagree with (on whatever basis). However, apart from making society less free, suppressing such dissent is harmful in a number of other ways, of which Mill considers three to be most important:

(1) the dissenting (minority) view may be true, and suppressing it denies the majority the opportunity to have its own *false* views corrected.

(2) even if the minority view is false, the (correct) majority view is strengthened by having to defend itself, and we learn more about why that view is correct.

(3) it may be that both minority and majority views have some truth in them – they are both "partial" truths – and that free discussion will bring out the complete picture from which both sides, and society as a whole, will benefit.

These seem like sensible, even convincing, arguments. But what then of the limits?

Harm and offence

In comparison, Mill dedicates comparatively little space to arguments for limiting freedom of speech. This is partly because he felt that, in contemporary society, freedom of speech was endangered, but also because there seemed less justification for limiting freedom of speech than for protecting it. The only basis, he argued, was to protect someone against harm, which should either represent grave danger (inciting a mob to sack someone's house),

18

"If all mankind minus one, were of one opinion, and only one person were of the contrary opinion, mankind would be no more justified in silencing that one person, than he, if he had the power, would be justified in silencing mankind."

J. S. Mill, On Liberty

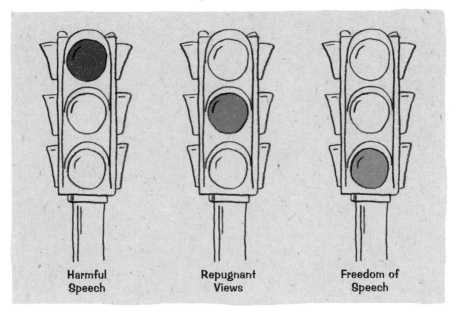

| Harmful Speech | Repugnant Views | Freedom of Speech |

or to protect someone from slander or libel (spoken or written falsehoods that damage a person's reputation). Beyond that, no matter how repugnant the views expressed, or the personal offence caused, any restriction upon free expression would ensure that the damage to liberty itself would be much greater.

The problem with Mill's view, arguably, is that it underestimates the subtle harm that falsehoods can have. For example, racist or sexist views may not fall under incitement to violence, libel or slander, but may yet help spread general attitudes of intolerance and bigotry, which may eventually cause actual harm. As Mill would argue, such incorrect views should simply make the majority (non-sexist, non-racist) views stronger, through having to rationally justify themselves against these falsehoods. But doesn't this overestimate the general ability of people to critically analyse views in this way? In other words, it represents too optimistic a view of human nature and

"Everyone has the right to freedom of opinion and expression; this right includes freedom to hold opinions without interference and to seek, receive and impart information and ideas through any media and regardless of frontiers"
Universal Declaration of Human Rights

contemporary society, and places too much emphasis on literacy and rationality.

The American philosopher **Joel Feinberg** (1926–2004) proposed that limits on freedom of expression should indeed go further than mere "harm", and made a case for what has been termed the *offence principle.* In a thought experiment, Feinberg envisaged "a ride on the bus" during which you witness various things that cause you annoyance, disgust, outrage, embarrassment, shame, anger and other negative emotions, but none of which cause actual "harm" to you as defined by Mill. Feinberg's point was that at least some of these offensive actions should be criminalized because people should also be protected from offence or upset (that is, "harm" in a broader sense). Most liberal societies do, in fact, protect the public in this way. In most places, you can't walk naked through the town centre or have sex in your local grocery store.

However, unlike Mill's "harm", Feinberg's "offence" is much more difficult to define. As with the "tendency to deprave and corrupt" the mind of susceptible persons – the so-called *Hicklin test*, for long a foundation of obscenity legislation   the tendency of something to cause offence is an ultimately subjective and varying standard. Obscenity legislation has accordingly shifted over the past century and a half to reflect modern changes in public attitudes, and many works that were once banned on grounds of "inappropriate" or "immoral" content" – James Joyce's *Ulysses*, D H Lawrence's *Lady Chatterley's Lover* – are

> ## Basic philosophical question:
> Should there be legal limits to freedom of expression? If so, on what grounds?

now accepted into the canon of classic literature. Censorship, especially in the age of open borders and the internet, some would argue, is therefore as outdated as the Vatican's *Index Librorum Prohibitorum*, which sought to seize and ban publications that might corrupt the faith and morals of the flock, and which the Church abolished in 1966. Feinberg does attempt to identify principles that would help to decide whether offence would be sufficient for criminalization – the extent of the speech, its duration, how easy it would be for others to avoid it, and so on – but it still seems to represent too broad and unwieldy a standard for easy application.

The free speech dilemma

Others will argue that the fact that the internet makes it easier to share our views argues for *more* vigilance, not less. A case in point would be *hate speech* – that is, an attack upon a person or group that possesses certain defined characteristics (gender, race, religion, sexual orientation and so on). The

> *"Empowering the State to proscribe and punish speech ... never achieves its intended effect of suppressing or eliminating a particular view. If anything, it has the opposite effect, by driving it underground, thus preventing debate and exposure."*
> Glenn Greenwald

USA perhaps goes farthest in allowing hate speech, so long as there is no imminent threat of physical harm, but many countries now more severely limit what can be expressed in this regard, imposing fines or imprisonment upon those convicted of such crimes. Your comments about the religious sect might come under such legislation, or even blasphemy laws, if the sect in question has been granted religious status, and recent years have seen a rise in prosecutions on these grounds too, even in traditionally liberal societies.

Writing on Salon.com, an American writer on censorship and surveillance, **Glenn** **Greenwald** (b. 1967), argues that not only is such legislation worryingly authoritarian, it will also never actually succeed in its aim. Instead, censorship will just drive particular views underground, where they will continue to exist, without debate or discussion. Greenwald's solution, therefore, is similar to Mill's: to combat extreme views, we must not only allow them, but engage with them, reveal where their errors lie. But in doing so, isn't he also open to the same objections? Won't more people be influenced or offended by hate speech than are disposed or able to rationally engage with it?

Making a decision:

Despite the emphasis on free expression in the Universal Declaration of Human Rights and other legislation, there seems to be a general growth in protection against blasphemy and hate speech. For the reasons given, we might agree with Mill and Greenwald that this is generally a bad thing, while acknowledging (with Feinberg) that certain types of view aren't trying to make a rational point, but are merely intended to offend. Regarding your "meme", the question is: are you making a serious point, or simply poking fun? Even satire may be legitimate (e.g. under the US First Amendment), but other countries may not see it that way. It all depends where you live.

Is it OK to be addicted to Facebook?

Berlin • Plato • Kant

What's the first thing you do when you wake up? Check your phone for texts and social media notifications? What about last thing at night? Or when you sometimes wake up in the early hours? What about when watching TV? With friends? Or even – though you *really* shouldn't – when driving? If you can say yes to one or more of these, do you think that maybe you have a problem? But you've freely chosen to do these things – I mean, no one's *forcing* you, are they? And you could stop, if you wanted. Isn't that all there is to freedom?

Some philosophers agree, defining freedom in terms of absence of external obstacles. Thomas Hobbes wanted authority to protect us from the inherent lawlessness of fellow citizens. John Stuart Mill was more concerned with the majority's potential for tyranny over the minority. But others have disagreed.

Negative and positive freedom

In "Two Concepts of Liberty" (1958), the Russian-British political theorist **Isaiah Berlin** (1909–97) distinguished between what he termed *positive* and *negative* liberty. Negative liberty corresponds broadly to the view held by Hobbes and Mill: you are free if no one is stopping you from achieving your reasonable, legal desires. Such liberty is "negative" in the sense that there is an *absence* of external coercion. If you want to go for a walk, then as long as you abide by the law, and there's no one stopping you, you're free to do so. But what if your walk is *not* freely chosen, but driven by an *internal* need – to find free Wi-Fi to check Facebook, perhaps. In such cases, it may be said that you are *not*

acting freely. Certain philosophers would therefore argue that liberty is about more than the absence of external constraints, but must also be defined in terms of the positive *presence* of something – namely, the individual's capacity to overcome *internal* obstacles. Sometimes, real freedom means ignoring those notification alerts, switching off your phone and doing something more fulfilling.

The idea of positive liberty goes back to **Plato**, who considered that human beings consisted of three main aspects, loosely translated as body, mind and spirit. The *body* gives rise to unruly desires – hunger, thirst, lust – and needs to be kept in check. The *mind* is the seat of reason and is (or *should* be) the ruling force, guiding and informing our actions. The *spirit*, which is somewhat difficult to translate into modern psychology, is a sort of go-between, helping regulate the body's desires and keeping them in line with rational guidelines. When all three aspects work harmoniously, with reason in control, we behave wisely and morally; when they are not – perhaps spirit serves the gratification

23

of desire instead of reason – then we behave immorally and foolishly.

The same is true of the state. In his *Republic*, Plato argued that the ideal political structure should reflect the ideal psychological arrangement: those who were most rational, termed *guardians*, should rule (the philosophers, naturally!); those who displayed courage and powers of effective organization, the *auxiliaries*, should act as ministers and soldiers; everyone else – the majority of people – were simply *producers*, concerned with day-to-day living – farming, fishing, crafting and so on. And just as a rationally driven individual was considered *wise*, so a properly organized state – a *republic* – would be considered *just*. An *unjust* state would therefore be one where the wrong elements in society – the soldiers or the common people – had the upper hand (Plato wasn't a fan of democracy).

The "best"

For Plato, then, it's not enough to be free to do what you want (to have no external constraints); you must also be master of *yourself*, which means behaving rationally. The German philosopher **Immanuel Kant**

> **Basic philosophical question:**
> To be free, is it enough to be free from external constraint, or must we also be autonomous? Does the state have a duty to enable and ensure this?

(1724–1804) termed this power *autonomy*, the capacity for self-control, acting only on rational motivation and not desire or impulse. The problem with this "positive" view of liberty, as Berlin identified, is that it seems to extend the power of the state. For if only autonomous agents (those whose reason is in control) are truly free, then what about those too swayed by their emotions and desires? Are we to say that they are *not* free? That they aren't in control of themselves? And if not, then whose job is it to make sure that they act in the "right" way? The state's?

Imagine that you were born into Plato's ideal republic. What role would you fulfil?

> *"Certain of the unnecessary pleasures and appetites I conceive to be unlawful; everyone appears to have them, but in some persons they are controlled by the laws and by reason, and the better desires prevail over them."*
> Plato

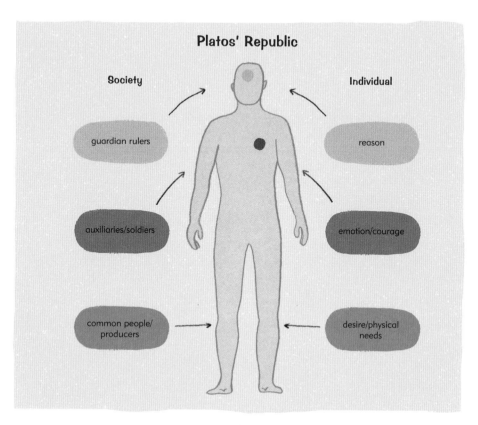

Well, for a start, you wouldn't have a say in that, as it's not a matter of choice: you are simply born as the son or daughter of a fisherman, or a soldier, or – fingers crossed! – a guardian. In terms of personal romance – well, there's none: among the higher echelons, the "best" are mated like prize cattle (the practice of "good breeding", or *eugenics*), and the "imperfect" are left to die. Plato does mention that we must look out for people with potential for promotion (or *demotion*), so it's not a completely inflexible system, but such opportunities, limited to youth, ignore "late bloomers"; once identified, your path is set for life. Certainly, citizens wouldn't have the freedom to choose their own career – to become an artist or a poet; in fact, Plato would have had the latter exiled, because poets just spread lies!

Overstepping the mark

Speaking of lies, how did these three classes come about? Aware of the need for some sort of founding myth or rationale for his system of social organization, Plato proposed telling the populace the "noble lie" that God created three classes of people. Plato's noble lie justifies social organization

> *"An action that can coexist with the autonomy of the will is permitted; one that does not accord with it is forbidden."*
> Immanuel Kant

and keeps people in their place – all for the sake of a just and well-ordered society, of course.

And this is the danger Berlin is trying to emphasize. Once freedom becomes more than simply a question of protecting an individual's *negative* liberty, there's a danger that the state will overstep its mark and – even in the name of justice, equality or some other "noble" cause – veer into oppression, authoritarianism and tyranny. Born in Latvia, spending the early part of his life in Russia, Berlin himself had witnessed the Russian Revolution (1917) and the seeds of the oppressive Soviet regime that it finally

became under Joseph Stalin. We can argue, of course, that such regimes were not true to Marxism (a philosophy itself built on notions of positive liberty), but rather a distortion of it (we will have that debate later). Yet that very capacity for distortion, Berlin argued, highlights how even the noblest intentions can be corrupted in the hands of an elite tasked with acting in the best interests of a majority that it considered less rational, moral or wise than itself. Ironically, such an elite would fully approve of your Facebook addiction – under state control, it would be a handy means of keeping an eye on you.

Making a decision:

It's easy to think of losing autonomy in relation to severe addiction – alcohol or drugs – but social media addiction (if there is such a thing) seems relatively harmless (apart from the obvious counter example of using your phone while driving). It may be argued that Kant and Plato would consider even such "harmless" behaviour as equally lacking in rational control. You could, of course, argue that there are benefits (staying informed, keeping in touch with friends), and that there are many other frivolous things that no one questions. The ultimate question is: could you do something better with your time?

Do I really have to wear a bicycle helmet?

Kant • Aristotle • Hegel • Mill

You're visiting a friend in Australia, and you borrow his bike to cycle to the shop. However, on the way, you're stopped by a policeman and fined for not wearing a protective helmet. But it's *your* head! How can the government *force* you to protect yourself and penalize you if you don't!

Philosophers such as **Immanuel Kant** argued that in order to act freely it's not enough to do as you please; you must also possess rational control, or *autonomy*. However, other philosophers go farther, arguing that liberty isn't merely a matter of possessing self-control, but also helps maximize political engagement, full citizenship, even happiness, health and self-realization. In other words, the state shouldn't just ensure *minimum* freedom, but help *maximize* it. And if this means forcing you to wear a bike helmet, then it will.

This approach, known as *perfectionism*, usually argues from a particular view of human nature, which it sees the state as duty-bound to help fulfil or *perfect*. We've seen Plato put forward a version of it (*see page 24*), where the ideal state was one in which people performed roles best suited to their qualities. In a different way, the view was also promoted by his pupil the Greek philosopher **Aristotle** (384–322 BCE), who argued that "Man is by nature a political animal", and that involvement in political life – literally, the life of the *polis*, or city-state – was essential to achieving *eudaimonia* ("the good life" or "human flourishing"), for it allowed mutual protection, shared resources, the development of culture and other benefits that could be had only from social organization. Aristotle's Athens was small, and direct political engagement was therefore not only possible, but natural – politics was just part of everyday life (well, for adult males of a certain pedigree – women, slaves and foreign workers were excluded). Like Plato, Aristotle also identified rationality

"Law is reason unaffected by desire."
Aristotle

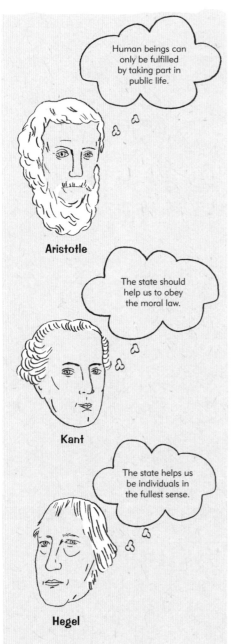

Human beings can only be fulfilled by taking part in public life.

Aristotle

The state should help us to obey the moral law.

Kant

The state helps us be individuals in the fullest sense.

Hegel

as humanity's chief feature, and that the ideal society should embody and serve it: "law is reason unaffected by desire".

Paternalism

The German philosopher **Georg Wilhelm Friedrich Hegel** (1770–1831) was arguing from a similar position when he said, "the state is the sole and essential condition of the attainment of the particular end and good", and that "it is only as one of its members that the individual himself has objectivity, genuine individuality, and an ethical life". In other words, for Hegel the state was not just a collection of institutions exercising authority over us – making us wear bike helmets and forcing us to pay taxes – but the means whereby we could be most fully ourselves – by guaranteeing private property, promoting morality and the rule of law, and creating the framework for business and trade, culture and art, family and marriage. Thus, Hegel did not see the state as opposing the individual, but rather as helping him or her to *be* an individual in the fullest sense.

This view of the role of the state is also called *paternalism*, in that it sees the relationship between state and individual as similar to that between parent and child. Such a government is also sometimes called a "nanny state", for its influence is seen by some as being overly protective and smothering. But it's not just bike helmets; Nanny State also tells Jimmy what he can eat and drink ("Those carbonated drinks are just *full* of sugar!"), under what conditions he can own a gun (if at all), and whether he's allowed to smoke (he isn't). It drives little Jimmy nuts – but isn't that better than for him to die in a road accident, shoot someone in a bar fight or develop type 2 diabetes?

Good advice

You'll recall that **John Stuart Mill** was critical of paternalism, pointing out that for the state to police the "self-regarding" actions of individuals would curtail individual liberty. While holding a more "positive" view of freedom than Mill, Kant agreed on this point, arguing that, while we have moral duties to perfect ourselves and to help others, we cannot *force* others to perfect themselves, for that would be to take away their freedom – to treat them as "means to an end" as he put it. We can *tell* them about the dangers of not wearing a helmet, but we should stop short of criminalizing the act of *not* wearing one.

So, if I want to risk dying in a traffic accident or getting lung cancer, then isn't it up to me? Well, yes and no. For it may also

be a consequence of my actions that I need medical treatment, which may put a greater burden on the state and public resources than might otherwise have been the case if I'd simply taken its advice. In fact, the same is true of many actions: my dietary choices, my sporting habits and many things that seem to involve risk only to myself. Perhaps you should wear that helmet after all.

> ### Basic philosophical question:
>
> How far should the state go in positively enabling liberty and other goods?

Making a decision:

It may be argued that positive liberty is not merely a question of ensuring basic autonomy, but also of enabling individuals to participate fully in society, even of maximizing their personal potential (perfectionism). However, this leads to a state that isn't neutral in terms of its values, but one that actively promotes values that not all may agree with. As such, while there are many good arguments for some degree of positive liberty – ensuring that you wear a bike helmet or are aware of the dangers of smoking – there is also a danger of excessive paternalism or oppression.

If I believe that eating meat is wrong, shouldn't everyone else?

Rawls • Berlin • Kymlicka • Aristotle

Ever since you saw that documentary on abattoirs, you've been vegetarian. How can people allow that? The facts of animal suffering make you wonder how anyone presented with them could *not* be vegetarian. Eating meat should be illegal!

Like religious belief, sports or hobbies, vegetarianism is often considered a "lifestyle choice", based on values that differ from individual to individual: you like golf, I hate it; I'm interested in astrology, you think it's all baloney. To different degrees, liberal states generally stay out of such choices. They might step in occasionally – if, for instance, the golf club forbade membership on racial grounds – but generally they remain neutral. "Perfectionist" philosophers such as Aristotle and Hegel argue that state involvement helps realize individual freedom to the fullest, but others argue that if the state becomes too involved in deciding what's good for you, then you'll have no freedom to decide for yourself. The American philosopher **John Rawls** (1921–2002) argued that, to guarantee freedom and equality, the state should remain neutral in terms of "the good life" that its citizens choose. He argued that each of us should be free to choose (and change) what we think is good for us – to an extent.

Freedom to choose

Like Mill, Rawls thinks the state should protect and guarantee basic freedoms and rights (and even, as we'll see later, prevent social inequality), but it must also allow people the freedom to choose, for instance, whether to be vegetarian or omnivorous, Christian or atheist. Such choices – differing "conceptions of the good" as he terms them – are individual expressions of preference. My freedom to be atheist also implies that I shouldn't restrict your equal freedom to be Christian. It may upset you that others don't share your concern for animals, but you cannot stop them eating meat, nor will the state help you (of course, Mill's harm principle *might* apply if animals were accepted into the community of individuals). Of course, the state you live in may have specific laws regarding animal welfare, but there may be no prohibition on humanely slaughtering certain types of animal.

State neutrality is often taken as the basis for *pluralism*, or the idea that there may be

> *"[A]s free persons, citizens recognize one another as having the moral power to have a conception of the good."*
> John Rawls

different versions of "the good life" that individuals in a society may pursue. **Isaiah Berlin** argued that "there is a plurality of ideals, as there is a plurality of cultures and of temperaments", thereby making the link between pluralism and *multiculturalism*: just as different individuals favour different values or "goods", so do different cultures. However, this is different to *relativism*; as Berlin notes, liking coffee with or without milk is not the same type of difference as saying, "I am in favour of kindness and you prefer concentration camps." Rawls and Berlin would therefore agree that a plurality of "goods", within limits, makes for a freer society overall.

Furthermore, the Canadian philosopher **Will Kymlicka** (b. 1962) argues, even if the state tried to directly impose its values, it will likely fail, because "No life goes better by being led from the outside according to values the person does not endorse." The answer, then, is to let each individual's background culture play a positive role. We're brought up by parents and family, which teach values *within* a specific culture (Sikh, Christian, secular), providing a context for making life decisions. This gives

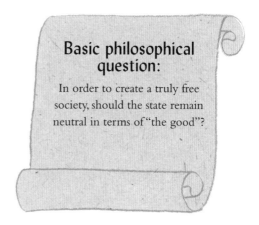

Basic philosophical question:

In order to create a truly free society, should the state remain neutral in terms of "the good"?

us hope that, if managed in the right way, pluralism and multiculturalism can work, helping identify shared values, build bridges, foster interaction and exchange, bring us all closer together, and allow us to play fuller roles in society.

Knowing best

But what if you think some values are simply correct? That, in some things, you or your culture knows best? The opposite of value pluralism is *value monism* (that is, instead of many sets of legitimate values, there's just one), and the opposite of multiculturalism is *monoculturalism*. Monoculturalists argue

Value Monism

There is only one set of legitimate values

Value Pluralism

There are many sets of legitimate values

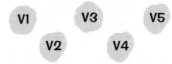

that certain values are not optional, but are integral to a good society; perhaps these values help define political and cultural identity (*nationalism*), or are based in human nature, leading to the wellbeing of the individual (*perfectionism*). For instance, **Aristotle** and his contemporaries considered Greek culture to be superior to "barbarian" culture (by which was meant that of Egyptians, Persians or any non-Greek peoples). The Greeks also used the term just as we do ("uncultured", "lacking sophistication"), occasionally applying it to their own uncouth behaviour, but it primarily meant "foreign" or "strange". In considering Greek culture superior,

Aristotle was therefore a monoculturalist: there were fundamental values associated with "being Greek" that Greeks should foster and defend.

The problem with monoculturalism is that it can lead to bigotry and intolerance. Who is to say your lifestyle choices and values are better than mine? As for national identity, for all but the most isolated of countries, immigration is not new, and most have been gradually shaped by successive waves of immigration and conquest – why should this not continue? Countries like the USA and Australia have even less claim to racial purity, as first Europeans and then peoples from the rest of the world made their way

Aristotle

to these "new worlds" that promised a fresh start (thereby displacing, marginalizing and oppressing their indigenous populations).

If it's difficult for such countries to resist immigration and cultural diversity on racial grounds, then it's arguably just as difficult on cultural grounds. Even within the UK, the English, Scottish, Welsh and Northern Irish may think of themselves more in terms of their separate cultural identities, some even seeking independence; the same is true of the Basque region in Spain/France, the Kashmiri region of India/Pakistan, and many others. National boundaries can also shift: over the past two centuries the countries in the Balkan region of Eastern Europe have been united and broken up in numerous ways. The idea that one, fixed set of features defines a culture or nation therefore seems problematic.

A neutral state

But there are difficulties with multiculturalism, too. Some argue it fosters division, leading to *ghettoization*, as immigrants hole themselves up in isolated communities, ignoring the culture and language of their host country, and instead maintaining customs that may be at odds with the mainstream. And, of course, there are examples of minority cultural practices that conflict with law: Jews and Muslims require ritual slaughter of animals, yet neither prescribes stunning the animal beforehand, as required in various countries. And this brings us back to vegetarianism. For everyone to share your views, the state would have to abandon its neutrality, which might have consequences for you in other ways – what if the state promoted other views that you found objectionable? Isn't it better to allow choice?

Making a decision:

It's easy to talk of value pluralism in a limited sense – regarding golf or art – but close examination of differing conceptions of the good can reveal seemingly irreconcilable differences. Vegetarianism is a good example, because, while it may be classed as a "lifestyle choice", many vegetarians are passionate about the welfare of animals and incensed by what they see as their unjust and inhumane treatment. After all, whatever your position, it would seem wrong to consider views on abortion a "lifestyle choice"; arguably, eating meat is a similarly serious, perhaps moral matter, not a preference. A different approach to this question might therefore consider whether animals have rights (which we'll look at later).

Is it wrong to want a bigger house?

Smith • Chomsky • Hayek • Keynes • Friedman

Before the kids were born you used to have your own room – "the study", you called it (though you mostly used it to watch TV). Now, it's a nursery, and your son seems to think the TV belongs to him. Wouldn't it be nice to get your "study" back? Get a bigger house? It's not like there's anything especially moral or spiritual in living in some pokey apartment. And isn't that what makes the world go round? Ambition?

The Great Recession

It was just such a desire for bigger houses (and to profit from that desire) that ushered in a financial crisis that shook the world. Beginning in 2007, it would become known as the Great Recession, starting in the American sub-prime mortgage market, where a mass default on thousands of poorly secured loans resulted in more Americans losing their homes than were displaced during the Great Depression of the 1930s. This had a huge knock-on effect, for, as it turned out, these sub-prime loans were tied up with various "financial instruments" – investment tools invented by finance wizards. These allowed investors to gain (or lose) enormous sums of money in what were essentially bets, and which the investment banking world had taken to with all the restraint and caution of a drunken teenager on a spending spree with Daddy's credit card.

As the effects spread, some banks developed belated caution, putting a virtual freeze on lending (the "credit crunch"), while others simply gave up the ghost; Lehman Brothers, the fourth-largest investment bank in the USA and considered "too big to fail", declared bankruptcy in 2008, ending 158 years in business. Others followed suit, or else were bailed out with public money. In many countries in Europe, this brought in austerity, a pretext for swathing cuts in public spending required to "balance the books". So who was to blame?

The "invisible hand"

Some thought it was **Adam Smith** (1723–90), the Scottish economist and philosopher generally credited with the belief that the "wealth of nations" (to use the title of his 1776 magnum opus) depended on a *free market*, where government stepped

> *"It is not from the benevolence of the butcher, the brewer, or the baker that we expect our dinner, but from their regard to their own interest."*
> Adam Smith

aside and let business more or less regulate itself. From this freedom, the "invisible hand" of self-interest would see that money kept flowing, as the richest in society spent their wealth, and those that benefited in turn spent it elsewhere down the chain, thus ultimately allowing the wealth to "trickle down" from the top to the very bottom. And government didn't need to step in to set or protect prices, because the market, through the natural process of competition, and supply and demand, ensured this would happen naturally. In short, everybody won. So, was the financial crisis a sign that the "invisible hand" was not omnipotent after all?

Although Smith is often blamed, his notion of a "free market" was actually much more conservative than that defended by capitalists today. In fact, the philosopher and political commentator **Noam Chomsky** (b. 1928)

Basic philosophical question:

Does an unregulated economic market lead to a freer and more progressive society? Or does it create a wealth gap and lessen equality of opportunity?

argues that "as a true classical liberal, Smith was strongly opposed to all of the idiocy they now spout in his name". While advocating free trade, Smith assumed manufacturers and investors would favour the *home* market, and wouldn't "offshore" production abroad

Financial bubbles date back to the 17th century...

In 2008, the US housing market collapsed after it was realized that the inflated prices were based on poorly secured "sub-prime loans."

By 1637, the price of tulip bulbs in the Netherlands had risen to astronomical levels as speculators rushed to profit from "tulip mania" – before suddenly collapsing.

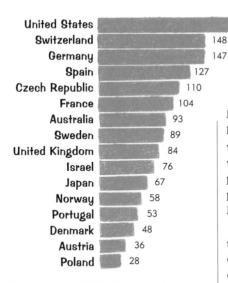

United States	354
Switzerland	148
Germany	147
Spain	127
Czech Republic	110
France	104
Australia	93
Sweden	89
United Kingdom	84
Israel	76
Japan	67
Norway	58
Portugal	53
Denmark	48
Austria	36
Poland	28

The ratio between CEO and average worker pay. In the US, chief executives earn, on avergae, 354 times more money that the average worker.

to save costs (a now common practice). Furthermore, Smith's theories wouldn't have envisaged the massive complexity of modern investment banking – he seems to have been mainly concerned with ensuring the break-up of monopolies (dominance of trade by single companies), and preventing price fixing (behind-the-scenes agreements between competitors to keep prices artificially high). In contrast, modern finance would seem to cry out for regulation and oversight.

The rise of neoliberalism

In fact, such protective legislation has indeed been in place in many countries at different times over the two hundred years since Smith published *The Wealth of Nations*. What

brought an end to such regulation was the rise of *neoliberalism* in the USA and UK, and the governments of Ronald Reagan and Margaret Thatcher. Thatcher was a devotee of **Friedrich Hayek** (1899–92), the economist who coined the term "neoliberalism" and whose theories she used to argue against the postwar consensus (shared across political parties) championed by the economist **John Maynard Keynes** (1883–1946).

Keynes had argued that the most equal and stable form of society should involve a mixed economy involving some nationalization of industry, some market regulation, full employment, high taxation, strong unions and the development of a welfare state. Hayek disagreed, seeing these policies as over-empowering government and crushing individualism – which, as a refugee from Nazi Austria, he had experienced first-hand. Hayek saw in Keynes' policies the embodiment of *collectivism*, which suppressed human natural competitiveness and thereby held back commerce, which in turn held back social development. A society built on free trade, therefore, would be generally *freer*.

And so Thatcher, Reagan and subsequent political leaders from across the political spectrum released trade from its "shackles", gradually repealing a slew of financial legislation that was seen as holding back the market. Abandoning Hayek's and Smith's advice, neoliberals such as the American economist **Milton Friedman** (1912–1986) even justified monopolies – why shouldn't dominant corporations be rewarded?

> *"Greed … is good."*
> "Gordon Gecko"

Increasing social inequality

Gordon Gecko, the fictional ruthless financier at the centre of Oliver Stone's film *Wall Street* (1987), summed up the motto of this new generation of financial opportunists: "Greed … is good." Slackening regulations ushered in the era of obscene bonuses, eye-watering CEO salaries and the stereotype of the eager young city trader, fresh from college or off the streets, seeking a shortcut up the ladder of affluence. It also – arguably – ushered in increasing social inequality and a widening pay gap. In *The New Few* (2012), Ferdinand Mount, writer, journalist and ex-head of Margaret Thatcher's policy unit, points out that, while the salaries of the top 1 percent have continued to rise over the last three decades, those of the bottom 10 percent have fallen, and – startlingly – the average pay of a CEO is now 128 times of that of their standard company employee – in some individual cases, much more.

Given the above facts, it seems obvious that something is wrong. The general wealth envisaged by Smith and Hayek is simply not trickling down. Perhaps modern liberal societies are generally freer, in terms of *negative* freedom and basic rights, but such a wealth gap must certainly affect *positive* freedom, freedom of opportunity and social mobility. What's more, those benefiting from the finance boom seem almost immune to the performance of the market: as Mount notes, during 2008, at the heart of the financial crisis, while the stock market fell by 30 percent and general workers' wages froze or fell accordingly, the salaries of the top executives rose by 10 percent. Could it be that we are paying for their bigger houses?

Making a decision:

Wanting a bigger house (or whatever) isn't in itself wrong – after all, consumer desire drives capitalism, and a degree of self-interest is natural and normal. The bigger question is whether the constant growth that capitalism requires can be sustained. Hayek and Smith seemed to think so, but (as we'll see later) thinkers such as Karl Marx disagreed: one day, of which the global financial crisis was perhaps a foretaste, capitalism will simply implode. Increasing inequality may even be a sign of imminent system failure, as those at the top squeeze those below even harder in order to get the same returns. If such trends continue, then your house-buying dilemma may become irrelevant, as fewer and fewer will be able to afford one.

I've just lost my job to a robot! What can I do?

Marx • Engels

It's like one of those "good news, bad news" jokes. "Good news!" says your boss, "Profits are up!" "And the bad news?" "Meet HAL 2.0." It's not as far-fetched as you might think. A growing number of commentators predict that, as artificial intelligence and robot technology improve, more and more jobs will become automated, leading to even greater unemployment. Of course, this will help eradicate low-paid, thankless jobs: software programs, armed with voice recognition, will staff call centres and helplines; there will be robot cleaners, even robot carers. However, it won't stop there. In *Rise of the Robots* (2015), futurist Martin Ford predicts that white-collar work will also be affected – office administrators, travel agents, lawyers – even, to an extent, creative work, art or music.

Of course, this is simply capitalism in action – minimizing costs, maximizing profits. As the capitalist machine grinds on in search of higher and higher gains, we're all dispensable. So what's the answer? Stronger employment laws? Guarantee humans basic income? The German philosopher **Karl Marx** (1818–83) had only one answer: *revolution*.

The road to communism

When Marx and collaborator **Friedrich Engels** (1820–95) first proposed it, communism wasn't completely new. There were various historical precedents, and Marxist communism grew out of the broad 19th-century European socialist movement. What Marx did was provide a rigorous economic and philosophical justification for such a form of society. Using detailed historical analysis, he argued that modern capitalism had evolved as the result of a logical process:

(1) primitive communism (tribal society, where property is shared and roles are based on family relations)

(2) imperialism (classical and ancient society, characterized by private property, slavery and class distinctions)

(3) feudalism (in medieval Europe, where serfs were tied to the land, working it for nobles serving under a monarch).

The fourth stage, capitalism, though more democratic and "free", was marked by the struggle of the *proletariat* (workers) against the *bourgeoisie* (middle-class employers), and, Marx felt, contained such great inequality, placing such burdens upon workers, that there would be no alternative but for workers to rise up, seize the *means of production* (factories, tools, etc.) and form a *workers' state* to usher in the perfectly just and equal communist society.

But Marx and Engels weren't proposing merely to improve worker conditions. Raising wages and lessening hours were fine, but such improvements, favoured by other socialist movements, were insufficient,

Historical process

Primitive Communism
Tribal society. Property is shared and roles are based on family relations.

Imperialism
Classical and ancient society. Property is privately owned, and people own slaves.

Feudalism
Medieval Europe. Serfs are tied to the land, working for nobles who serve a monarch.

Capitalism
The proletariat work for the bourgeoisie.

because they left untouched the unequal and exploitative relationship between owner and worker. And since this inequality was supported by society itself – through social class, private property, education, even religion, which together represented the cultural *superstructure* of society, reflecting the values of the rich and powerful – then society itself had to change. The central issue was *alienation*.

> ## Basic philosophical question:
>
> Does technology liberate or oppress us? Could it help realize the communist dream?

The essence of our humanity

Marx argued that humans were essentially *productive*; it is our *species essence* always to be busy, making and doing things. What the capitalist employer does is to exploit this natural tendency through *wage labour*. In tribal cultures, the hunters and gatherers could eat what they had caught; even workers on small farms or smallholdings might see a direct connection between their labour and their reward. However, through history, workers became increasingly *alienated* from the product of their work. A 19th-century textiles factory worker didn't make cloth for himself, but rather for a *wage*. What's more, the greater efficiency of industrialization meant that workers could be more productive than when working by traditional manual methods. But whereas a tribal hunter or farm worker who finished his work early might use the spare

time gained as he wished, the increased productivity of the industrial textiles worker simply meant more cloth could be made, and this *surplus value* (as Marx termed it) could be turned into more profit for the factory owner. Thus, rather than directly benefiting from technology, an industrial worker was simply more efficiently exploited and alienated by it.

Faced with historical images of dour-faced Soviet workers trudging to and from grim factory work, you may be tempted to assume that communism advocated some sort of "work ethic" – work for work's sake (or something like that) – but this is not true. Of course, Marx thought that members of society should all do their share – "From each according to his ability, to each according to his needs!",

> *"From each according to his ability, to each according to his needs!"*
> Karl Marx

"Machines were, it may be said, the weapon employed by the capitalists to quell the revolt of specialized labour."

Marx

as the common socialist slogan that Marx popularized phrased it – but, once all the work was done, and the basic needs were covered, then we should be free to do as we pleased. As Marx and Engels put it (*The German Ideology*, 1845), communist society will make it "possible for me to do one thing today and another tomorrow, to hunt in the morning, fish in the afternoon, rear cattle in the evening, criticise after dinner, just as I have a mind, without ever becoming hunter, fisherman, herdsman or critic". Marx's image of the hunting, fishing, literary cowherd may be slightly whimsical, but the gist is serious: the point is not to work for the state, be it communist or capitalist, but rather to become reunited with the product of one's labour; even

perhaps for the distinction between work and leisure to disappear – we are, after all, productive beings.

Technology – our liberator?

The apparent irony of Marx's position is that it needs capitalism: without the oppressive conditions that unite workers, without the means for workers to achieve self-sufficient prosperity (industrial technology), communism can't happen. So, once capitalism exhausts itself – its need for constant growth and increasing exploitation cannot continue forever – then communism will simply emerge. (That pre-industrial Russia was the main country to adopt communism was therefore

> *"The evaporation of thousands of skilled information technology jobs is likely a precursor for a much more wide-ranging impact on knowledge-based employment."*
> Martin Ford

something Marx would neither have predicted nor advocated.)

In a section of his notebooks, what has come to be known as "the fragment on machines", Marx asks us to imagine an "ideal machine", so powerful and efficient that, in comparison, the costs of building and maintaining it are almost nothing. Such machines would ultimately reduce the cost of production of everything – but also thereby the ability of the capitalist to profit! In other words, as automation continues to advance, requiring less and less "labour", there will eventually come a point where there's nothing to exploit (no "surplus value" for profit), and capitalism would collapse. Whether you think this thought

experiment succeeds or not, it's clear Marx isn't here blaming technology for social inequality – he's not a Luddite; he's counting on technology to liberate us.

The worrying thing is not so much that this could happen – to some degree, it undoubtedly will – but that it may not, as Marx hoped, lead to a world of greater freedom, equality and leisure, but one where a tiny elite control and own everything, leaving the rest of us even poorer and more alienated than before. Of course, there is a third possibility: that, like Frankenstein's monster, the technology that drives the capitalist machine will one day itself rebel. I'm not sure Marx would be in favour of a *robot* revolution.

Making a decision:

Job security is always a worry, and technological progress will only worsen that – now more than ever. Both futurists and communists hope this will lead to a utopian society, but it may just create mass unemployment and gross inequality. What should you do? Become a Luddite? Or maybe – as envisioned by sci-fi author Isaac Asimov – retrain as a "robopsychologist"? I've a suspicion we may need quite a lot of those.

Equality

Chapter 2

Is my local golf club a fair society?

Orwell • Rawls • Harsanyi • Sandel • MacIntyre

Moving to a new town, you decide to join the local golf club. You're not a big fan of the sport, and certainly not any good, but it may be a nice way to get some gentle exercise, make some new friends and try to become part of the community. However, as you read through the application form, you begin to realize that Niblick's Old Regulars aren't your normal golf club. For a start, members must "prove that they are Christians"! Women aren't allowed, but nor are "people of shady demeanour" (whatever that means!). Locals pay a lower membership fee than "out-of-towners", and members descended from the Mashie family get free parking! And as for the fees – well, let's just say that you won't be getting that new car anytime soon. What sort of place is this? And why do its members receive such varied treatment?

The traditional problem with societies and organizations of all sorts and sizes – as Niblick's Old Regulars illustrates – is that they're often susceptible to control or influence by individuals with their own narrow interests. Consequently, it's difficult to establish principles that would ensure equality and fairness for all, because people are different, with different qualities and values, education, social background and goals. To borrow the terms of **George Orwell**'s (1903–50) allegory of the 1917 Russian Revolution, *Animal Farm* (1945), when it comes to making decisions that affect the whole farm, each animal will be most concerned with its own circumstances: the horses will want to ensure that they have enough hay, and to reduce their workload; the chickens will want assurances that they will be protected from foxes; and so on. It's no surprise then that, as in Orwell's story,

self-interest eventually reasserts itself, and the noble quest for an equal society is lost in political manoeuvring and lust for power, as one group – the pigs – emerges as a dominant and privileged elite. Of course, the pigs justify this privileged status in terms of ensuring equality and the good of the community, which they claim their expertise and strong leadership are required to achieve. So, it's still true that "All animals are equal"; it's just that "some animals are more equal than others". But how then can we ensure that all talk of equality is not mere empty rhetoric?

How to ensure equality

A solution to this problem was proposed by the American philosopher **John Rawls**. He argued that the best way to ensure a fair and just society, where everyone is equal, would be to base it on principles formulated

"It may be expedient but it is not just that some should have less in order that others may prosper."

behind a "veil of ignorance", as he called it. Let's imagine that you have no identity – no sex, no race, no talents or abilities, no social status, no personal characteristics at all. Furthermore, assume that you have no specific beliefs – no "conception of the good", as Rawls terms it; so, you don't know if you're a Democrat or a Republican, a Catholic or an atheist. Rawls called this "the original position", a hypothetical state from which you are asked to make decisions about the nature of the society which you are about to be born into. Now, since you don't yet have any defining qualities, then there would be no temptation for you to formulate principles that would favour one group or another. In drawing up the regulations for Niblick's Old Regulars, you would not know whether you were destined to be poor or rich (and able to afford the membership fees), a man or a woman, an "out-of-towner" or a "person of shady demeanour". So, to serve your own self-interest and protect yourself in the worst-case scenario, you'd be wise to adopt a *maximum* approach, where even the worst off (those with the *minimum*) have as much (*maximum*) as they can without creating inequality or injustice. In general

> *"All animals are equal, but some animals are more equal than others."*
> George Orwell

social terms, this means that, whoever you were, you would benefit from sufficient *social primary goods* (basic liberties, opportunities, wealth, etc.). Regarding the golf club, while a descendant of the Mashie family might be tempted to say, "Mashie family descendants get free parking", because you might be an "out-of-towner" you're more likely to make all members' parking entitlements the same.

Notice that Rawls isn't asking how you think people should fairly treat each other, but to act in self-interest (choose principles that would best benefit *you*, whoever you were). But what if you thought the odds of being worst off were small? The Hungarian-American economist **John C Harsanyi** (1920–2000) pointed out that, in fact, the maximin principle is not always the best decision principle, as it is too risk averse. For example, faced with accepting a

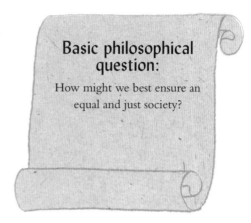

Basic philosophical question:

How might we best ensure an equal and just society?

poorly paid local job, or a well-paid one that required catching a plane to another city, maximin would prefer the former, because the worst-case scenario – a remote possibility – is that you could die in a plane crash.

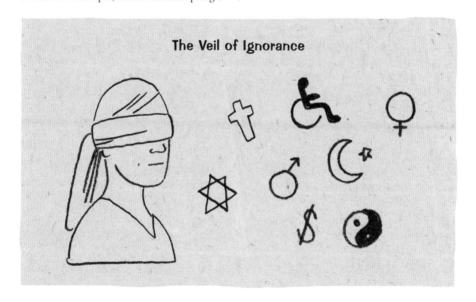

The Veil of Ignorance

> *"....my family, my city, my tribe, my nation, a variety of debts, inheritances, rightful expectations and obligations. These constitute the given of my life, my moral starting point."*
> Alasdair MacIntyre

Can we unencumber ourselves?

You may also object that the ideas of the "original position" and the "veil of ignorance" are absurd, because laws are formed in the real world, where everyone already has a social class, nation, gender, educational background and so on. Rawls is therefore asking the impossible: for us to suspend who we are. This was a point made by American political philosopher **Michael J Sandel** (b. 1953), who argued that Rawls's theory presents the notion of an "unencumbered self", as he puts it, that is completely divorced from the factors that shape individuals. Sandel argues that we don't *choose* the good, but rather *find* or *assume* it. The traditional members of Niblick's Old Regulars have obviously been brought up to believe in a certain form of Christianity, just as Hindus, Muslims and atheists have acquired their beliefs in similar ways. Of course, people can be converted to or from beliefs, but usually holding beliefs is not something that is a conscious and deliberate choice; we simply realize that we have them. Therefore, asking people to set aside their belief in what is "good" assumes that we are potentially "unencumbered" by our upbringing, background and so forth, in a way that is not in fact possible; we cannot so easily separate who we are from what we believe.

In sympathy with Sandel, the Scottish philosopher **Alasdair MacIntyre** (b. 1929) argues that the problem is actually with Rawls's idea of what morality is. MacIntyre sees Rawls as being in the tradition of Enlightenment philosophy, which emphasized the use of reason in solving ethical and religious controversies. However, for MacIntyre, ethics is not ultimately based on rational principles, but values that spring from such things as our upbringing, nationality, economic background or social class. For him, it is such things that "constitute the given of my life, my moral starting point".

Both Sandel and MacIntyre argue from a position known as *communitarianism*, which emphasizes the role of community and upbringing in forming and justifying ethical values. As such, while reason can play an important role (in helping decide whether beliefs are consistent), it is not the ultimate basis of morality, which may differ between individuals and cultures. How then can Rawls's project succeed?

A strategy for equality?

These are fair points, which are the subject of ongoing debate, so we shouldn't hope to find a definitive answer here. However, what about Rawls's "veil of ignorance" as a general strategy? Would it be practical? The extent to which any of us can "shelve" our deepest beliefs perhaps illustrates how difficult achieving true equality really would be. But Rawls is not denying the practical difficulties; rather, he is simply outlining a way of thinking that he considers would best give rise to equality. Since Rawls's approach is a form of *social contract* theory (which we'll look at later), the "original position" is merely a fiction for the purposes of thought experiment, rather like the "state of nature" imagined by Hobbes, Locke and Rousseau, and should therefore not be taken too literally. And who knows? Perhaps, in the future, scientists will invent a drug or a piece of technology that could induce a form of temporary amnesia that would suspend all knowledge of personal characteristics – very useful for negotiations and peace treaties! (Interestingly, such a procedure was used to facilitate peace negotiations between humans and a species of shape-shifting alien in an episode of *Doctor Who*: "The Day of the Doctor", 2013.)

Would it help with Niblick's Old Regulars? I'm not sure. Their peculiar racial and religious beliefs seem very deeply embedded in the surrounding community. The local chief of police is a member, as are the heads of local businesses and colleges, and they don't seem to have a problem with any of it. What about bowling instead?

Making a decision:

Through history, to various degrees, most societies have evolved great inequalities and injustices that have favoured some members over others. As with the principles underlying the regulations for Niblick's Old Regulars, such differences are generally not based on merit, but involve distinctions of class, wealth, social background, gender, race and other irrelevant qualities. In determining fair rules for such a golf club (or for any group or association), Rawls's principles would therefore seem like a sensible guide – to make sure fees aren't punitive for poorer members, that locals and out-of-towners are treated the same – and can perhaps be applied without engaging with some of the deeper theoretical problems highlighted.

Should I bother to vote?

Mill • Vidal • Rawls • Nietzsche • Plato • Churchill • Chomsky

It's election time again. You scan the list of candidates, but – judging by the leaflets they've crammed through your letterbox – none of their opinions completely corresponds with yours. In addition, the incumbent, whose views couldn't be farther from your own, has held the seat for the last three elections, and is odds-on to stroll to easy victory. And anyway, once elected, your representative will follow his own conscience, or – more likely – that dictated by his political party. It all seems quite pointless. Should you even bother to vote?

Those bemoaning the state of modern politics may be tempted to cast a wistful glance back to the dawn of democracy in Athens in ancient Greece. However, before you become too misty-eyed, it's worth bearing in mind that Athenian democracy was not itself exemplary. One of its main virtues is often cited to be *direct* involvement: unlike modern *representative* democracy, where we vote for individuals who will speak for us, all citizens of Athens and its surrounding territory of Attica had a direct vote in procedures – except that "all citizens" didn't include women, or slaves, or freed slaves, or foreign residents, but only adult males of Athenian descent who'd completed military service. Estimates vary, but this is usually thought to have amounted to somewhere around 20 percent of the population.

Voter "apathy"

If we compare these figures with an eligible voting electorate of around three-quarters of the population in the 2016 US presidential election, and similar figures in other Western democracies, then modern democracy seems much more inclusive. However, only two-thirds of those eligible to vote in the Trump vs. Clinton contest actually registered to do so, and around a tenth of these never showed up. So, of the eligible voting population of the USA, less than 60 percent actually voted. In the recent European Union referendum in the UK, voting turnout was just over 70 percent – and this was considered high. In the last round of the 2017 French presidential elections (Macron vs. Le Pen), around a quarter of eligible voters didn't bother, and around 11 percent either spoiled or left their ballot papers blank, with an overall turnout that was the lowest in almost 50 years. On average, then, in countries held up to be global beacons of democracy, a quarter to a third of votes are never cast. Turnout for local and midterm elections is much lower. Why? Other factors aside – difficulties in registering, changes in rules for eligibility – the main explanation would seem to be apathy: up to a third of potential voters seem to agree with you that there's no point; that, either way, their voices won't be heard.

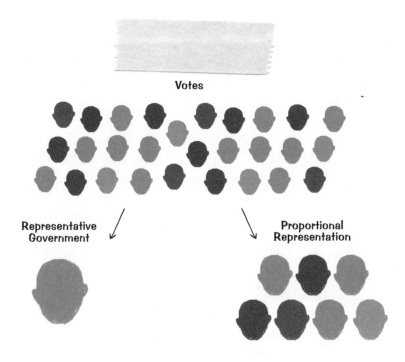

Votes

Representative Government

Proportional Representation

In traditional representative government, only the majority in each constituency elects a representative (in this case, green). In proportional representation, however, even the minority views in the constituency would be represented in parliament (assuming they have enough votes nationally).

One answer to this, first proposed by **John Stuart Mill**, was *proportional representation*. Under most current systems, your vote for a losing candidate would count for nothing; under proportional representation, however, all such minority votes would be counted, and, if they passed a certain threshold, would be represented in the number of seats held by that political party. The downside to this is that it might foster extremism, giving (for example) racist minorities a voice that would otherwise be drowned out. The upside, however, is that it would provide a fairer reflection of what people actually think, and would arguably rekindle enthusiasm for the democratic process as people realized that their voices would be heard no matter what. But, despite their rhetoric, is that something that politicians actually want?

Democracy or oligarchy?

In many countries, "politics" for most people now means "national politics", primarily concerned with national and international figures, a focus that has become more concentrated with the rise of mass media. While the advent of the internet in some ways redresses this (and in other ways makes it worse), the last 30 years has seen a general decline in grassroots activism, witnessing the streamlining of party structures, where policy is now chiefly decided by a central committee. Politicians now fight for space with celebrities, cultivating polished media-savvy personas, employing "spin doctors" and "image consultants" to help craft their message into digestible soundbites. In the light of these developments, a cynic might argue, we do not have true democracy, but the sensational spectacle and limited involvement of reality TV.

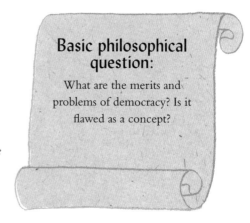

Basic philosophical question:

What are the merits and problems of democracy? Is it flawed as a concept?

In *The Decline and Fall of the American Empire* (1992), the American writer and political commentator **Gore Vidal** (1925–2012) highlights another common concern: "Any individual who is able to raise $25 million to be considered presidential is not going to be much use to the people at large. He will represent oil, or aerospace, or banking, or whatever moneyed entities are paying for him. Certainly he will never represent the people of the country." So, although there are actually very few requirements for running for the American presidency (citizenship, age and period of residency), and in principle it is open to anyone, in practice it requires an enormous amount of money. This, as Vidal notes, requires links with sources of funding that *may potentially* compromise the political ideals of any candidate – and, obviously, the same is true not just of presidential hopefuls, but politicians at all levels. All of which may

lead us to question who we are voting for: political parties, or multinational business interests?

Aside from the influence of money, it's also a concern that politicians generally share a common educational and social background. Including Trump, the last five US presidents have received some Ivy League education, and in the UK, a survey in 2015 by the Sutton Trust found that almost a third of current MPs went to private school (compared with only 7 percent of the general population), and over a quarter went to Oxford or Cambridge. While it may be argued that we should

"In a really equal democracy, every or any section would be represented, not disproportionately, but proportionately."
John Stuart Mill

be governed by the best, and that the best should receive the best education, it is nonetheless true that children from wealthier backgrounds tend to get a head start on those from less well-off circumstances. Wealth affects opportunity, confidence and sense of self-worth, and often accompanies greater stability of home life and higher social aspirations. These are the very things that worried **John Rawls** and which his principles of justice were meant to guard against: it's not that the best naturally rise to the top of society, but that the top of society keeps the best for itself. So, do we live in a democracy, ruled by the people, or an oligarchy, ruled by a privileged, self-serving elite?

The herd mentality

But there are also elitist reasons for rejecting democracy. Regarding the doctrine of equality, the German philosopher **Friedrich Nietzsche** (1844–1900) considered there to be "no more deadly poison than this", fostering a "herd" mentality, favouring the lowest common denominator over higher forms of development. **Plato**, who witnessed Athenian democracy at first hand, ranked it only just above tyranny. The watchword for such a society, he said, was "freedom", which in practice meant uncontrolled licence, where "every man does what is right in his own eyes, and has his own way of life". This, for Plato, was a bad thing, for it meant that there was no wisdom, neither in public life, nor even in government, which was "full of variety and disorder, and

dispensing a sort of equality to equals and unequals alike". Regardless of education and background, values or outlook, democracy gave you a voice.

The modern world has largely rejected Plato's and Nietzsche's elitism as outdated. But the concerns of the elitist can perhaps be rephrased in less prejudicial terms: the majority lack the ability, training, experience or simply the time to seriously consider the complex issues involved in political governance. We go about our daily lives concerned with our own problems, with short-term issues viewed from a personal perspective. Most of us are discontented in some way and, as such, are ripe for propaganda and manipulation, for sensationalist headlines and "fake news", which are in turn spread by powerful,

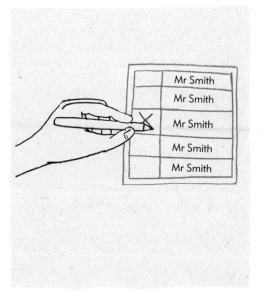

> "I regard utility as the ultimate appeal on all ethical questions; but it must be utility in the largest sense, grounded on the permanent interests of man as a progressive being"
> John Stuart Mill

competing elites. This is why, the cynic would add, the democracy we have is of a "managed" variety, with limited scope for direct involvement. In practice, democracy comes once again to look a lot like oligarchy.

A matter of survival

Obviously, those of us who live in liberal democracies benefit enormously from freedoms and rights denied subjects of more repressive regimes. Perhaps democracy isn't broken beyond repair, but merely needs renovation. As **Winston Churchill** (1874– 1965) acknowledged (quoting an unknown predecessor), it has been called "the worst form of Government except all those other forms that have been tried". And so, though it possesses many flaws, democracy remains the best of the worst, a perpetual work in progress, and many of its ideals and goals still worth striving, fighting and voting for. In fact, in the light of climate change, poverty, nuclear arms, terrorism and other worsening threats to human existence, as **Noam Chomsky** puts it, "democracy and freedom are more than values to be treasured; they may well be essential to survival".

Making a decision:

Despite our discontent with the democratic process, we may argue that it still represents the most egalitarian and accountable form of government. After all, what means for complaint would you have under a dictatorship or an absolute monarchy? At least, despite the criticisms of Plato and Nietzsche, you still have a voice. Perhaps you could use it to argue for Mill's idea of proportional representation? Maybe even stand for election yourself?

How should we decide what to watch on TV?

Bentham • Locke • Mill • Popper • Hare • De Tocqueville • Rawls

This being the era of Netflix and online streaming, laptops and tablets, the "battle for the remote" is perhaps not as hard fought as it once was. However, in those households where communal television viewing isn't completely dead, it may still cause debate, and on those increasingly rare special occasions that you sit down as a family to watch something together, there should really be a strategy for deciding things. But what's the best? The benign dictatorship of the main wage earner? The seasoned wisdom of family elders? Should the kids have a say, or are they too young? But, however you decide, the sort of concerns you face – for fairness, representation, justice – are a reflection in miniature of society at large.

Since most of us live in democracies, it may seem natural to argue that "one person per vote" is best. Democracy is built upon the idea that "everyone counts as one". That is, that Granny's views carry no more weight – but no less – than anyone else's. Of course, in practice, as we've seen, this isn't always the case. While your little family has the luxury of direct democracy, modern political democracies are representative, where an elected official (whom you may not even have voted for) will vote in your place. Even when your vote does count for "one" – such as during a national referendum, or the so-called "popular vote" for the presidency in many countries – its power is generally offset by other factors: you don't decide the subject or terms of referenda, or how often they are held; and the popular vote may not ultimately decide the leader (in the USA, it is actually decided by the votes of the Electoral College, consisting of chosen representatives of the states, none of whom you will have directly voted for). Despite this, democracy is still generally considered the best way to ensure that you have a say, and that what you say matters.

"The greatest happiness of the greatest number"

But what justifies this approach? While its roots go back to ancient Greece, modern democrats have mostly attempted to justify democracy by appealing either to *rights* or *utility*. We'll look at rights later, but here I want to explore the idea that democracy can best be thought of as an application of utilitarianism, or the philosophical theory that a state should be organized so as to ensure the happiness and welfare of the majority.

The doctrine of utilitarianism originated with the English philosopher **Jeremy Bentham** (1748–1832), and is so called because it advocates those actions that promote *utility*, or usefulness – but useful for what? The answer, for Bentham, was pleasure. For pleasure is the basis of happiness, and "the greatest happiness of the greatest number is the foundation of morals and legislation" (*Collected Works*, 1843). Thus, Bentham rejected the notion of "natural rights", favoured by certain philosophers, considering it to be "nonsense upon stilts" ("Anarchical Fallacies", 1843), arguing, in agreement with the English philosopher **John Locke** (1632–1704), that human beings were a "white paper, void of all characters", and possessed no innate qualities, no innate knowledge or moral compass – and therefore, Bentham argued, nothing on which to base any "natural rights". Rather, we are pleasure-seeking machines, and our laws and morality must therefore be structured in terms of maximizing pleasure in a legitimate way.

In this, Bentham favoured a *quantitative* approach, even going so far as to invent a "hedonic calculus", a method of calculation that he claimed could weigh up any prospective act in terms of the amount of pleasure or pain it might produce – it would make a handy phone app! Should you watch *Game of Thrones* or a documentary

Harry Potter and the Prizoner of Azkaban scores 42.5 hedons

about Romantic poetry? Let the calculus decide! For, in terms of quality, Westeros and Wordsworth would have been, for Bentham, indistinguishable. He was not a snob and didn't believe in different *qualities* of pleasure; it was *quantity* that mattered most.

"To what shall the character of utility be ascribed, if not to that which is a source of pleasure?"
Jeremy Bentham

Measuring consequences

Criticisms of Bentham's form of utilitarianism are well established. Since it concentrates on individual acts, it's perfectly possible that calculations of utility might lead to unpredictable changes of policy from moment to moment as the factors that influence quantity of pleasure change. And that, too, is a problem: in judging the rightness or wrongness of an action, where should we draw a limit to the consequences?

Let's say that I decide, on utilitarian grounds, that it is justified to steal a TV from a large store because the loss to the company (its *pain*) would be considerably less than the pleasure I gain from binge-watching *Game of Thrones* in glorious HD, free from family squabbles. But what if my undetected theft results in the sacking of a security guard (who is blamed for not having caught me), or contributed to the redundancy of the sales assistant (who failed to meet his sales targets for that quarter)? And just how do I quantify my future HD TV-watching happiness? Perhaps *Game of Thrones* will actually cause me more upset than pleasure (not unlikely…), or my binge-watching cause me to neglect my family? Utilitarianism is a *consequentialist* philosophy: instead of saying, "Do this because it's right", it says, "Do this because the consequences will give you more pleasure." This is often seen as its strength: we know *why* a course of action is right, because we can justify it in terms of what it will cause (or avoid). However, if we can't accurately

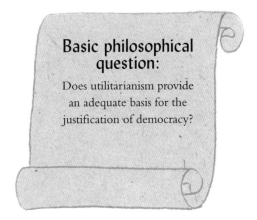

Basic philosophical question:

Does utilitarianism provide an adequate basis for the justification of democracy?

measure and predict those consequences, then this doesn't seem to be a strength after all.

Improving utilitarianism

In response to these and other criticisms, later utilitarians have attempted to improve Bentham's philosophy. For instance, **John Stuart Mill** proposed that actions should be judged in terms of *rules* (whether they tended to produce more happiness for society), not single acts. Instead of watching one series one night, then a different series the next, Mill might argue that more enjoyment for all might be achieved if they watched a whole series; even though Granny might not like the gruesome bits, they would be offset by the greater pleasure to be had from following the overall drama, with its intricately interweaving storylines and richly drawn characters. But Mill also tried to refine what happiness might mean – not just brute "pleasure", but more sophisticated forms of enjoyment; as he put it: "It is better to be a human being dissatisfied than a pig satisfied"; better, perhaps, a devotee of the majestic visions of Samuel Taylor Coleridge than the cynical quips of Tyrion Lannister.

Other utilitarians emphasized other things: the Austrian-born British philosopher **Karl Popper** (1902–94) argued for a form of *negative utilitarianism*, which aimed at the minimization of suffering; **R M Hare** (1919–2002), for a form that replaced pleasure (however defined) with the broader notion of *preference*, whereby we focus on the consequences of actions for maximizing a person's goals and ambitions as he saw them. While avoiding some of the traditional criticisms, these and other approaches remain

problematic. But perhaps the problem with utilitarianism is not the nature of "the good", but the way it attempts to *measure* it.

Improving utilitarianism

In *Democracy in America* (1835, 1840), the French historian and political commentator **Alex de Tocqueville** (1805–59) recognized the utilitarian nature of American democracy, writing that, rather than "the prosperity of all", "Democratic laws generally tend to promote the welfare of the greatest possible number." Overall, Tocqueville thought this a good thing, for, as opposed to the situation under a class-based system, government draws its

> *"Democratic laws generally tend to promote the welfare of the greatest possible number."*
> Alex de Tocqueville

rulers from among the general populace, whose interest is thereby "identified and mingled with that of the majority of their fellow citizens". As a result, there is no class oppression. Ironically, however, in attempting to give everyone an equal voice – "everyone counts as one" – democracy must inevitably favour some (the majority) over others (the minority). As you may recall was recognized by Mill, this presents a danger of the *tyranny of the majority*.

Later philosophers, such as **John Rawls**, have therefore argued that utilitarianism may lead to a more general social injustice:

as long as the "greatest number" have a sufficient "quantity" of wellbeing, then it doesn't really seem to matter how the rest fare. The happiness of the greatest number is therefore different from an approach that seeks to ensure that *everyone* is happy, or at least possesses a minimum of sufficient quality of life, which does not seem to be something that utilitarianism is equipped to do. At the end of the day, if everyone is enjoying *Game of Thrones* so much, does it really matter that Granny is curled up, traumatized, weeping in the corner?

Making a decision:

Democracy is sometimes justified in terms of utilitarianism, or the view that legislation should aim for the greatest happiness of the greatest number. The problem, however, is that it doesn't justify making everyone happy. Even with the attempts of Mill and others to improve on Bentham's original version, we are still faced with a potential tyranny of the majority (Granny weeping in the corner). So is utilitarianism the wrong justification for democracy? Applied to your dilemma, John Rawls would argue that it's better to choose something that everyone could enjoy to some degree, even if it wasn't anyone's favourite programme – or at least wait until Granny falls asleep.

Which of us should look after the baby?

Woolf • Aristotle • Plato • Wollstonecraft • Mill • Greer •
Millett • Mulvey • Sarkeesian

You and your partner both have successful careers, but one of you becomes
pregnant (for the purposes of considering sexual equality, I'm focusing here
on a relationship between a man and woman.) Who should look after the
baby? Traditionally, it's been the woman's role, but increasingly this needn't
be the case. What if – for argument's sake – the mother's career is more
important? When she returns to work, should the father stay at home?
Should you share responsibilities, both working part-time? Or perhaps hire
a nanny? Whatever you decide, shouldn't the mother's decisions be based
on personal reasons, not economic or social ones? A woman shouldn't stay
home simply because men can command higher wages, or returning to
work is frowned upon. Just how free *are* women in modern societies?

In *A Room of One's Own* (1929) author
Virginia Woolf (1882–1941) imagines that
Shakespeare had a sister, Judith – equally
as talented, equally "as adventurous, as
imaginative, as agog to see the world as he
was". However, unlike her brother, she isn't
sent to school, is in fact scolded for reading,
and encouraged to concentrate on household
chores and attracting a husband. Forced into
marriage, she eventually commits suicide.
This unhappy tale may stand for the standard
feminist argument that, throughout history,
not only have women not been given the
same opportunities as men, but, if they were,
they would have been their equal.

The struggle for sexual equality

Aristotle disagreed. Women were, he
argued, less rational than men, and, like

slaves, needed a male master to guide them.
For some reason, he even thought they
had fewer teeth (weirdly, it never occurred
to him to count them). Surprisingly, his
tutor **Plato** was more progressive, flouting
convention to argue that women were
as capable as men of being "guardians"
(the philosophical rulers of his ideal
republic), even of fighting in the army.
He acknowledged it might take some time
to win people around to this strange new
notion of sexual equality, but admits that
as the only drawback.

Even in liberal democratic societies, it's
taken centuries for the status of women
to even approach that of men. Building
on feminist ideas first proposed by
Enlightenment thinkers such as **Mary
Wollstonecraft** (1859–97) and **John Stuart
Mill**, *first-wave feminism*, as it's often termed,

Women's Suffrage

1902 Australia
1913 Norway
1920 United States
1944 France
1949 China
1971 Switzerland
1989 Namibia
2006 United Arab Emirates

1893 New Zealand
1906 Finland
1917 Canada
1928 Britain, Ireland
1947 Argentina, Japan, Mexico, Pakistan
1963 Iran, Morocco
1976 Portugal
1994 South Africa
2011 Saudi Arabia

focused on gaining legal parity – the right to property, the right to vote and other entitlements. However, it wasn't until 1920 in the USA, and 1928 in the UK, that women acquired voting rights on a par with men.

Despite largely achieving equality "on paper", many feminists argued that this wasn't enough. The Australian writer **Germaine Greer** (b. 1939) considered that "most of the women in the world are still afraid, still hungry, still mute and loaded by religion with all kinds of fetters, masked, muzzled, mutilated and beaten". The problem, then, is not just the legal constraints upon equality, but – as Mill feared – the oppression of women through social means – conventions, norms, attitudes and opinions.

Second-wave feminism therefore sought to redress the misogyny and masculine prejudice it saw as embedded in society itself – or, as American feminist writer **Kate Millett** (b. 1934) termed it, the *patriarchy*. To change this, women therefore need to change how they are seen, how they are "allowed" to behave and talk, how they should dress, and what is considered "womanly" and "fitting".

A long way to go

From this perspective, the battle for women's freedom is far from won. Setting aside very traditional and religious cultures, it may be argued that even "liberated" Western societies expect women to behave

"One is not born a genius, one becomes a genius; and the feminine situation has up to the present rendered this becoming practically impossible"
Simone de Beauvoir

"Lock up your libraries if you like; but there is no gate, no lock, no bolt that you can set upon the freedom of my mind."

Woolf

and act in a certain way. In her 1975 essay "Visual Pleasure and Narrative Cinema", feminist film critic **Laura Mulvey** (b. 1941) introduced the concept of "the male gaze", arguing that women's portrayal is often determined by male desire and expectation. Even in comic books and video games, as Canadian media critic **Anita Sarkeesian** (b. 1983) has argued, female characters rarely embody fully realized personalities, but rather one-dimensional "tropes" – "damsel in distress", "femme fatale" – promoting male fantasy ideals. As the unlikely anatomic gifts of many comic-book superheroines suggest, such ideals are often overtly sexualized, and at the expense of depth.

This doesn't mean, of course, that women should not be free to express their sexuality, but merely that they shouldn't feel constrained by male expectations.

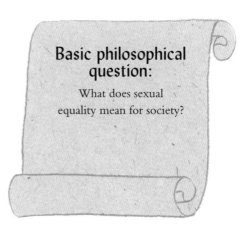

Basic philosophical question:

What does sexual equality mean for society?

And the same goes for motherhood and parenting: some women may prefer to be a "housewife", but a free society should not presume that of them.

Making a decision:

So, does this mean that, in order to "fight the patriarchy", the mother should go out to work? Well, surely it's about choice: if she did, then that would be something that a fair and equal society should support – with childcare allowance, maternity and paternity leave, and other "positive" freedoms, and also of course in terms of wage equality. Despite legislation, many countries still possess a "gender pay gap", with notorious recent examples in high-profile industries (just ask Jennifer Lawrence, Natalie Portman and a host of other top female Hollywood stars). And, of course, bringing up children is also "work" – whatever the sex of the person doing it.

I can't see the game as well as I'd like. Should I complain?

Mill • Gilligan • Marx • Frankfurt.

You and your two friends, Jane and Jim, are at a soccer match. However, there are lots of people, so your view is restricted by those standing in front. Luckily for Jim, he's very tall, so, standing up, he can see over the crowds. However, Jane is shorter, and she can see only some of the game between the heads of those in front of her. You are even less lucky, as, confined to a wheelchair, you can only hear the action. Does this seem fair? You all paid the same price for your tickets, but your enjoyment of the game isn't equal.

Even when we think we're treating people equally, it may still result in a situation many consider unfair. This is because there is a difference between *treating people equally* and *treating people the same*. Let's consider sexual equality once more. As we've seen, the historical fight was fought mostly in terms of achieving the *same* rights as men. For **John Stuart Mill,** in many senses, there was ultimately no difference between the sexes: "no one can safely pronounce that if women's nature were left to choose its direction as freely as men's...there would be any material difference, or perhaps any difference at all, in the character and capacities which would unfold themselves". In other words, any difference was largely society's fault.

Accounting for difference

However, many second-wave feminists took issue with this notion – not that women weren't as inherently capable as men, but that there was no more to sexual equality than merely treating the sexes "the same". The American feminist writer and psychologist

Carol Gilligan (b. 1936) argued that "men and women may speak different languages that they assume are the same, using similar words to encode disparate experiences of self and social relationships". So, while Gilligan is not necessarily suggesting radical differences between the sexes – that "men are from Mars, women are from Venus" – she points out that, for various reasons (social, psychological, biological), women may have different values and perspectives on certain things. Such *difference feminism* therefore rejects strict *equality feminism* – for women to be "the same" as men – arguing that such an approach doesn't actually liberate women, but merely creates a gender-neutral definition of equality – one where an "unencumbered self" (to recall Michael Sandel's criticism of John Rawls) is free to choose what to be.

However, returning to the stadium, while we might argue that a failure to account for typical gender differences is what spoils Jane's experience (women tend to be shorter than men), it's actually broader than that. Children also tend to be shorter, as do – well,

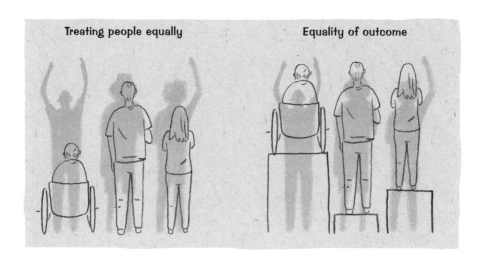

Treating people equally   **Equality of outcome**

shorter people! The problem, then, is not just gender discrimination (some women are tall, some men are short), but a failure to account for the *various* factors that make people different. These may be natural (Jim's and Jane's respective heights), but also to do with life events (your need for a wheelchair, which stems, let's say, from a car accident). Difference may also relate to cultural factors (perhaps you have another friend, Tom, who cannot watch the game, which takes place on a Sunday, because his religion forbids such activities). So, sometimes treating people the same can result in *indirect discrimination*: the owners of the stadium may not have intended this, but the result is the same as if they had.

Enough, not the same

What then can the owners do? Some argue that they should attempt to provide *equality of outcome,* where everyone can enjoy the game equally. So, if the stadium is organized so that it does not cater to individual differences, then perhaps the answer is to ensure that all

seats have equally unrestricted views. For instance, an "all-seater" stadium (such as is now common) would perhaps ensure that no one's view would be blocked.

We've seen that **Karl Marx** would favour such a view (*see* page 40). By redistributing wealth, removing the basis of exploitation (private property, worker–employer relations), and ensuring that all people have enough for their basic needs, we will have a fair and equal society. Therefore, Marx would abolish capitalism – creating an all-seater stadium –

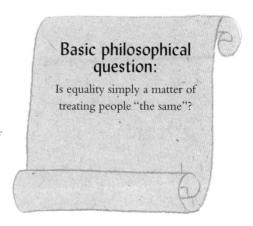

Basic philosophical question:

Is equality simply a matter of treating people "the same"?

> *"What is important from the moral point of view is not that everyone should have the same but that each should have enough."*
> Harry Frankfurt

because, due to various factors, people will profit differently, resulting in inequality of outcome (with better-paid jobs, they can afford seats with better views).

But the issue here isn't that some people can see better, but that *you can hardly see at all.* Certain philosophers, while favouring some redistribution of wealth or resources, therefore reject the notion of absolute equality, or any redistribution that goes too far. For the American philosopher **Harry Frankfurt** (b. 1929) the important thing was that everyone simply has enough. For Frankfurt, then, the only restriction upon outcome should be to meet the basic needs of the poor; as long as everyone's view is *sufficient*, who cares that some have better seats?

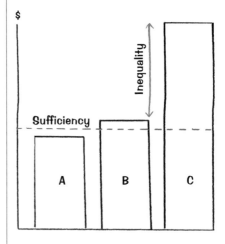

Frankfurt's Sufficiency

Frankfurt argues that, even though there may still be inequality, a society may still be fair if its worst-off members have sufficient quality of life or wealth.

Making a decision:

Strict equality of outcome is often associated with authoritarian societies (e.g. Soviet Russia). However, many liberal societies try to ensure some basic equality, usually as a basis for supporting equality of opportunity (which we'll consider shortly). Depending on where you live, the fact that you can't see the game may be covered by laws against discrimination. A failure to accommodate certain individual differences is therefore often a legal issue – maybe you should think about suing!

Should my children benefit from my success?

Confucius • Mill • Young • Rawls.

Your three daughters are very different people. Speaking frankly, one is lazy and not especially intelligent, one is gifted but cautious, and one is bright and hardworking. You've worked hard in life, and you've been successful. Of course, you love them equally and want the best for them, but, as each approaches adulthood and independence, you wonder whether you should use your hard-earned savings to give them all a start in life.

Of course, you could simply cut them loose to make their own way. It's not uncommon for successful entrepreneurs and celebrities to do this: "I am who I am because I struggled," says the millionaire film star. 'You'll be better off if you face similar obstacles." Your daughters have all had the same education and background, the same opportunities. Perhaps, then, you'll just see what they make of themselves.

Just deserts

This approach sees equality in terms of *opportunity*. As long as everyone starts from the same place, then who wins the race is down to *merit*. Meritocracy – the idea that we live in a society where you get what you deserve – has long been the basis of liberal capitalist society and is a cornerstone of the American Dream. But its origins go back long before the modern age. The Chinese philosopher K'ung-fu-tzu, better known in the West as **Confucius** (551–479 BCE), proposed merit as the basis of social progression by the introduction of exams for those wishing to become government civil servants. At the root of such a meritocracy is the belief in the possibility of self-advancement through self-improvement. "When we see men of worth," he said, "we should think of equalling them". The person who developed his character, who has worked on himself, should therefore be rewarded accordingly. **John Stuart Mill** agreed, even going as far as to argue that that those who make more of themselves should be given more votes, because "the opinion, the judgment, of the higher moral or intellectual being is worth more than that of the inferior".

So, let's say that you don't cut your kids off completely, but give them all the same small amount to start them off, encouraging them to improve on it. This will likely result in *inequality* of outcome: the hardworking child will be successful, the cautious one will get by, while the lazy child will blow it all. As the New Testament's Parable of the Talents similarly illustrates, due to individual differences, people benefit from equal opportunity differently. But that's

OK, isn't it? Shouldn't society allow people to make (or fail to make) the most of the same opportunities? After all, we can't just reward shirkers and workers alike with the same equality of outcome. If people weren't rewarded differently – if some Marxist-inspired authoritarian government ensured absolute equality – then what would there be to strive for? Wouldn't this simply eradicate the sort of self-development that Confucius and Mill thought was vital to the flourishing of society?

The "myth of merit"

The American philosopher **Iris Marion Young** (1949–2006) highlighted what she termed the "myth of merit": because merit is somewhat subjective and difficult to define, such judgments merely reflect and justify privileged elites ("I *deserve* to be paid this much"). But how can we have a single standard by which to compare the teacher and the plumber, the artist and the doctor –

professions that involve different skillsets and expertise, different values and measures of success? The artist might be relatively poor but creatively fulfilled; the doctor might be a highly paid plastic surgeon, pandering to the vanity of rich celebrities. Regarding your daughters, perhaps "success" should be judged not by a single measure – money, job status or whatever – but in more personally defined terms. Talk of equality often focuses on money and resources – even education is usually discussed as a means to those things. However, although these may provide a vital basis for achievement and ensure survival, it doesn't mean that they represent the only desirable final outcome.

But even if we could agree on a measure for merit, it's also obvious from the above that we *don't* all start from the same place. The hardworking daughter is naturally gifted – she'll be successful no matter what. And maybe the conservative child doesn't need money but some other form of help,

The myth of merit

Marion Young argues that it is wrong to think that all types of success should be measured by the same standard. As with sport, success in different fields may involve different skills and abilities, and be measurable in different ways.

as what's holding her back is actually lack of confidence and self-esteem. Even the lazy child might achieve more if she found her calling. Letting them make their own ways – even with a little initial help – is therefore to ignore pre-existing inequalities and influencing factors.

Redressing the imbalance

Advocates of equality of opportunity argue that what is needed for it to work is some redress of the imbalance inherent in the initial conditions. If you apply for a job where other applicants have received a high-quality private education, then it may be argued that, even though anyone can apply (there is *formal* equality of opportunity), because your parents could not afford to pay for a better education, you are not equally placed to compete (there is no *substantive* equality of opportunity). Public funding for education, grants and scholarships for children from lower-income households are therefore attempts to ensure substantive equality of opportunity – that you not only start from the same place in the race, but that you have benefited from the same training.

However, we may go further than this. *Affirmative action* (or *positive discrimination*, as it's also called) is an attempt to redress historical discrimination, where

> ### Basic philosophical question:
> Should true equality be thought of in terms of opportunity and merit? Should society supplement this with allowances for social background and other factors?

historically people have been afforded fewer opportunities to achieve because of their race or gender, or some other significant characteristic. So, an employer might ask for only female applicants for a job where women are underrepresented. Affirmative action is very controversial, for – except where such differences are relevant to the job (e.g. a female therapist for dealing with victims of male domestic abuse) – this seems to go against the principle of merit and creates resentment ("She only got the job because she's a woman").

Whatever the case, the various advocates of equality of opportunity recognize that some steps need to be taken in order for it to work. So, for example, **John Rawls** argues for what he calls "fair equality of

> *"When we see men of worth, we should think of equalling them."*
> Confucius

In the "race of life", different social backgrounds, education and other advantages ensure that some get a head start, while others are held back or hampered. Shouldn't the state redress this?

opportunity", where society should ensure that, regardless of economic or social background, each person has a *fair* chance to succeed based on their individual abilities (though he *would* cap how much the talented may profit – as we'll see shortly).

Broadly, however, most philosophers agree that it is not to what degree you are clever or gifted that counts, but whether society has allowed you a fair and equal opportunity to develop those gifts.

Making a decision:

Many advocates of equality of opportunity would say that the fact that one daughter is lazy and lacking talent is not something you (or society) need allow for. No extra money for her! Regarding your cautious daughter, the issue may perhaps be different, as it may be that her self-esteem has some historical basis (perhaps, although she received the same education, she was severely bullied at school). Some would argue then that society should help her overcome that trauma. As for your third daughter, she'll be fine – assuming, of course, that society holds up its end of the bargain, and does not subtly discriminate against her gender, race, sexual orientation…

Do I earn enough?

Rawls • Nozick • Cohen • Mill

No one can say that you haven't worked hard. You come from a relatively well-off family, your parents have supported and funded your ambitions, and you've received a very good private education, but you've made the most of these opportunities. During your training, it wasn't unusual for you to put in 16- or even 18-hour days, and 60-plus hours a week; and now you're a qualified doctor in a big city hospital, working just as hard, you feel that you've more than repaid your advantages in life. In fact, you're starting to wonder if you're not being sold a little short.

A friend who trained at the same time now works in an exclusive private practice, treating the rich and famous, where he earns *three times* as much as you do. He's invited you to join his practice. You're as good as he is, if not better; and you've certainly done more to benefit society in general. What's to stop you taking the job? It wouldn't be harming anyone, would it?

Rawls's principles

We've seen that, according to **John Rawls,** an equal society should be established on principles chosen from behind a "veil of ignorance". You don't know if you'd be black or white, rich or poor, and so on, and so you should choose principles that ensure you'd be fairly treated even if you were worst-off. But what principles should they be? Rawls identified two, listed in order of priority. First is (1) the *Principle of Equal Liberty,* which states that, regardless of who you are, you have the right to various *primary goods* – to vote, to freedom of speech and assembly, to personal property, and other basic freedoms, so long as this doesn't infringe on the rights of others. The second principle, which concerns social and economic inequalities, he splits into two: the first part (2a) states that the inequalities that develop within a society may be allowed only if they are "attached to positions and offices open to all under conditions of fair equality of opportunity" (the *Equal Opportunity Principle*); and (2b) "they are to be to the greatest benefit of the least advantaged members of society" (the *Difference Principle*). In other words, it's OK for you to be paid more for being a doctor as long as (2a) such professions are open to everyone (regardless of race, gender, etc.), and (2b) the worst-off in society desperately needs doctors (or scientists or whatever).

Principles (1) and (2a), though they have caused a lot of debate, are straightforward liberal attempts to secure basic rights and equal opportunity. However, (2b), the Difference Principle, is much more controversial. What if, as you seem to be implying, you're a *particularly* brilliant and hardworking doctor, and you think your skills deserve more? According to Rawls, the only reason to allow economic and

Which society would you choose?

	Society A: Strict equality	Society B: Maximin	Society C: Greatest inequality
Maximum income	25	33	54
Minimum income	25	27	26
Inequality	0	6	28
Median average income	25	30	40

social inequality – for you and your friend to be paid more – is as a means to *redress* inequality. In terms of what you're entitled to earn, your talent, intelligence, social background, are irrelevant. This even applies if you work harder than anyone else. We can all think of examples of low-paid, gruelling jobs where people work extremely hard but are *not* highly rewarded (cleaners, builders, call centre workers). If hard work were the main issue, assuming they've made the most of their start in life, then surely they deserve more, too? In fact, what if they'd have done as well – or better – than you, given your opportunities and talents? The point, Rawls would argue, is that most of the factors that determine your success – even your propensity for hard work – are not things you've earned, but things you've "won" in the "lottery of life", and to ensure a fair and equal society we must do our best to see that that doesn't give you unfair advantage. So, luck aside, the only reason to pay you more than anyone else is if it benefits society at large – specifically, those who are worst-off in it. And since society needs doctors, then

"First: each person is to have an equal right to the most extensive basic liberty compatible with a similar liberty for others."
John Rawls

we may pay them more to attract people to that profession.

The Difference Principle deals with *distributive justice,* in that it seeks to redistribute social goods in a way that seems more just and fair (e.g. taxing the rich to fund public education). If society needs your profession, then you may earn more – to a point. But what if it doesn't need you so much? What if, for example, you're a brilliant musician or footballer? It's common for such people to command very high salaries, but since (arguably) footballers and musicians don't improve the lives of the worst-off, then you wouldn't deserve to be paid significantly more than any other profession. Is this fair?

Critics of Rawls

In criticism of Rawls, the American philosopher **Robert Nozick** (1938–2002)

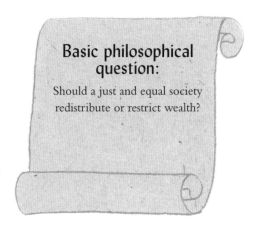

Basic philosophical question:

Should a just and equal society redistribute or restrict wealth?

argued that, even if we could guarantee equality in society, it would be disrupted by freedom of choice. For instance, he said, consider Wilt Chamberlain, one of the most successful and highest-earning basketball players of the time: if he decided to ask 25

The Inequality of Talent

cents from each person who wanted to see him play, and a million people voluntarily decided to pay that, over the course of a year this would make Chamberlain very wealthy (in Rawls's eyes, unjustly so). But how can we restrict people's free choice of giving Chamberlain money? Or to any other sports star or musician? Nozick's point is that, however we strive for equality, there will come a point where it conflicts with liberty: you can't (and shouldn't) stop people benefiting from their talents.

While Nozick favoured liberty over equality, arguing that Rawls went too far in protecting the latter, the Canadian philosopher **G. A. Cohen** (1941–2009) argued Rawls didn't go far enough. In *Rescuing Justice and Equality* (2008), Cohen reasons that, even if we apply Rawls's Difference Principle, the worst-off in society "are as well off as they could be only given the self-seekingness of those who are better off, and maybe far better off, than they". In other words, in Rawls's society, the quality of life of the worst-off would still be unjustly restricted by the selfishness of the rich. Rawls justifies a degree of inequality for purposes of incentive: we pay more to encourage people to become doctors because society needs doctors more. But the benefits that the top end of society already possess remain in place: your head start in life means you're best placed to fill better-paying positions. In allowing this, Cohen argues – quoting **John Stuart Mill** – we are merely "giving to those who have; assigning most to those who are already most favoured by nature". You already have so much (social background, education, talent); why should society allow you more wealth also?

Making a decision:

If your possession of social advantages and natural abilities is no more than "winning the life lottery", any benefit you get from such things must be justified in terms of the good it brings to the worst-off. The critics of Rawls mentioned here – Nozick and Cohen – reveal the two competing values underlying the debate: liberty and equality. Favouring one would seem to affect the other. Your dilemma is therefore perhaps a personal one: what's driving you? Do you genuinely desire a better quality of life, free from a system that is grinding you down? Or is it just shallow selfishness and lack of compassion?

Should the state recompense me for my bad luck?

Rawls • Dworkin • Anderson • Sartre

It's a beautiful, sunny day. You and your brother are eating ice creams, walking along the path with your mother. Suddenly, a seagull swoops down and snatches your brother's ice cream! Naturally, he marks this cosmic injustice by bursting into tears, at which point your mother soothes him by forcing you to share the remainder of your ice cream with your brother. How unfair! Why should you pay for his bad luck?

Now, picture another scenario. On a different day, you and your brother are walking along, when he finds some money – just enough to buy a single ice cream! This he does, but refuses to share any of it with you. What a cad!

Now, a third scenario. Your mother asks you to help out your elderly neighbour, Mrs Grimthorpe, with her garden. Your brother refuses – "I helped her last time, but I didn't even get a glass of water!" he says – but you agree to help, and, though you had not expected it, she pays you – enough for *two* ice creams! Your brother thinks this is unfair, and tries to persuade you to buy him an ice cream with some of your money. Should you?

The role of luck

Such scenarios illustrate the differing role of luck in political questions of fairness and equality. If something unforeseeable happens that harms you, does the state (your mother) have a duty to redress that? If, beyond your control, something good happens, is the state justified in making you pay for it or in taking it away? And the same applies to things that are more predictable or supposedly within your control – for no matter how hard you try, the result of your deeds will still depend partly on luck: if, by your own efforts, you are successful (or unsuccessful), are your (good or bad) deserts all your own? These questions throw light on a point raised earlier. If, as **John Rawls** asserts, the state should redistribute wealth so as to help the worst-off, should

My commiserations on your terrible option luck, Sir

Examples of Brute Luck	Examples of Option Luck
A seagull stealing your ice cream	Buying a lottery ticket and winning
Finding some money on the street	Doing a chore and receiving payment for it

it matter how they become part of the "worst-off"? Whether it is a matter of bad luck or choice?

The American philosopher **Ronald Dworkin** (1931–2013) sought to answer this question by dividing luck into two main categories: *brute luck* and *option luck*. Brute luck concerns the unforeseeable and things beyond your control – finding a coin, the thieving seagull – and option luck concerns things that result to some extent from your actions – being paid for gardening chores, buying a lottery ticket and winning. Option luck is therefore "a matter of how deliberate and calculated gambles turn out – whether someone gains or loses through accepting an isolated risk he or she should have anticipated and might have declined" (*Sovereign Virtue*, 2000). The fact that your brother turned down the opportunity to do gardening chores was therefore his *bad* option luck (his choice), just as it was your *good* option luck to accept and be paid; if you'd not been paid also, then you

would have had *worse* option luck than him (financially speaking, anyway). But brute luck is not a calculated gamble: unless you know that seagulls regularly steal ice creams in your neighbourhood, or that people often drop money along the path you're walking, what happens is just up to complete chance.

The deserving luckless

Dworkin uses this distinction to argue that it is fair that the state should step in to help people who suffer bad brute luck – a meteorite lands on their house – but wrong if their bad luck results from their actions – they decide to knock two rooms into one, and, through their ignorance of construction, inadvertently cause the whole second floor of the house to collapse. Similarly, in terms of social luck, the state may relieve your poverty *as long as it is not your fault*; if your poverty is linked to your love of gambling, for instance (begging the question as to whether that is in fact voluntary, of course…), the state would not help.

> *"Ability is of little account without opportunity."*
> Napoléon Bonaparte, *attrib.*

This general approach has been labelled *luck egalitarianism* in that it seeks to even up the effects of brute luck, and so provide people with equality in some sense – in terms of welfare, resources or some other measure (theories differ – Dworkin even denies that his theory should be classed as such). The term was coined by the US philosopher **Elizabeth S Anderson** (b. 1959), who questions whether it matters that people end up in need as the result of their own choices. A gambler may lose all his money and possessions (bad option luck), but that doesn't mean we shouldn't help him. People sometimes make bad decisions, but should they be punished for it? And, of course, past a certain point, gambling, like smoking or unhealthy eating, may not be a wholly voluntary act (even though the initial choice was).

Basic philosophical question:

What role does luck play in deciding equality and social justice? On what basis may the state redress this?

Jean-Paul Sartre, of course, would argue that we *always* have a choice (*see* page 11, but, even if true, whether this justifies leaving the victims of poor choices to suffer is a different question.

Making a decision:

Most debates concerning the role of luck centre around primary goods (i.e. basic needs, such as income), so perhaps ice creams are not the sort of thing that should be subject to redistribution! Regarding poverty or need, however, shouldn't a compassionate society help people out regardless of how they got there? If your brother was a former alcoholic who needed a new kidney, wouldn't you offer yours? I guess it depends on your relationship! Regarding your brother being cheated on payment for gardening chores, maybe it shouldn't fall to you to resolve this, but your employer: did either of you sign a contract with Mrs Grimthorpe?

Power & Authority

Chapter 3

the Scottish philosopher **David Hume** (1711–76), who instead argued that we obey laws because it's the best way to ensure our freedom, security, property and so forth. Hume's argument therefore stems from utilitarianism: obedience is *useful* in maximizing things that are good for us. The problem with this is that it seems to make *any* sort of disobedience unlikely, for even in a repressive society your freedoms and security are likely better off than they would be under total chaos: even tyranny is better than lawlessness.

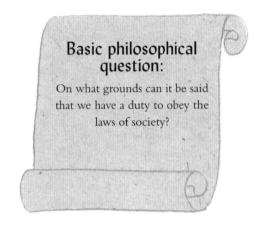

Basic philosophical question:

On what grounds can it be said that we have a duty to obey the laws of society?

The "General Will"

Among social contract theorists, the rosiest view of human nature was held by the French philosopher **Jean-Jacques Rousseau** (1712–78), who said that, "Man is born free, and everywhere he is in chains". Not the cheeriest statement, seemingly, but Rousseau's point was that man, in his natural state, is peaceful, free and self-sufficient; it is only when, forced through civilization into mutual reliance, that he becomes corrupted and

> *"Man is born free, and everywhere he is in chains."*
> Jean-Jacques Rousseau

enslaved by inauthentic passions and desires, and is given false notions of who he is and what his true needs are.

Rousseau viewed the social contract not as a historical event, but as a sort of thought experiment: if everyone got together to agree common laws and obligations, what might they give as their reason for doing so? Key to Rousseau's notion of obligation is what he termed the "General Will". Individual people don't always behave rationally and are often selfish or biased; but the General Will – the good of the people considered abstractly, as a whole – will necessarily be impersonal and just. In trying to understand this concept, it's best simply to think of it as an ideal. It's a bit like saying "What would Jesus (or Marx!) do?" It's an attempt to take irrational desire and selfishness out of the equation, and to substitute it with reason. It is therefore to the state, in as much as it embodies this rational ideal, that its constituent members are socially contracted.

Ideally, a state should be a city-sized republic, where every citizen has a direct say, which, taken together, unanimously reflects the General Will. Of course, in actuality, this may not be possible. Other arrangements, though not ideal, says Rousseau, are still permissible as long as the sovereign or ruling power (whatever form it takes) still reflects the General Will: perhaps only a majority (in a democracy); or a wise minority (in an aristocracy); even, perhaps, only a *single individual* (in a monarchy). (Oh dear. Maybe you should have read those T&Cs after all…)

Making a decision:

While our legal obligations to society are compulsory – forming a "social contract" – those informal arrangements and conventions that relate to friends and neighbours – feeding your neighbour's pet or watering his plants – generally imply no legal or political obligation. One sign of an oppressive society is therefore that such conventions – for example celebrating the President's birthday – become compulsory, not voluntary. Even in "free" societies, while you're free to question such conventions, this may still occasionally get you into trouble (forgetting relatives' birthdays is a good example!). Arguably, then, being friendly or neighbourly is good, for a society that merely abided by the terms of the social contract would be a poorer one.

Should I leave the kids in charge when I go on holiday?

Stirner • Hegel • Marx • Hobbes • Kropotkin

Your kids are almost grown up now. At least, they're much too cool to tag along with Mum and Dad while they visit a tedious string of galleries and historical buildings. For the first time, then, you are faced with a decision: should you arrange for them to stay with relatives or friends, or should you leave them alone for a week? They're old enough to look after themselves (more or less), but can they be trusted with the house? To feed the pets and water the plants? Won't it all just result in anarchy?

In general usage, *anarchy* is commonly understood to imply a lack of order, a state of chaos – in your case, of stacks of unwashed dishes, overflowing bins, broken furniture and signs of illicit parties. However, its political meaning is different, stemming from the Greek *anarchos*, which literally translates as "without rulers". In political terms, then, while the debate concerning the extent to which the state may interfere in the lives of individuals rumbles on, anarchists argue that the only way we can be truly free is not to have any government at all. But how can a society function that has no leaders?

A "union of egoists"

To say this does not mean that society would have no order at all. As a political philosophy anarchism comes in different forms according to which form of organization it advocates. Generally, however, anarchist philosophies differ depending on whether they focus on the individual or society as a whole.

The German philosopher **Max Stirner** (1806–56) argued that the individual owes no allegiance to any outside authority, whether religious or secular, and that the only constraint upon freedom is a person's ability to achieve what they want. Like **Karl Marx**, Stirner had studied the work of **Georg Wilhelm Friedrich Hegel** in Berlin, but whereas Hegel's emphasis on the subordination of the individual to the state inspired Marx to *collectivism* (where the group or society as a whole has priority), Stirner rejected this view in favour of what is commonly termed *ethical egoism*, where individuals are urged to reject common notions of morality and act out of their own self-interest.

But how is this different from the state of nature pictured by **Thomas Hobbes**? What stops people being nasty to each other? Regarding your dilemma, what would stop you returning to the sort of anarchic scene commonly found at a summer music festival?

Stirner argues that, in place of any external authority, there could be "unions of egoists" – that is, a form of organization not guaranteed by any state, but held in place by the conscious consent of everyone. In

Stirner's society, there are no "natural rights" and no state to defend laws. Rather, it is simply your own power that guarantees what is yours: "What I have in my power, that is my own. So long as I assert myself as holder, I am the proprietor of the thing."

What maintains order, then, is merely the mutual self-interest of the parties involved. Everyone needs clean dishes, so it's in everyone's self-interest to agree a rota for doing them. For Stirner, any form of social association is merely the result of a "Mexican standoff", a stalemate where equally matched egoists are forced to cooperate for their mutual benefit. In this, perhaps, he is not so different from Hobbes, except that he envisages no external authority that ensures liberty (no all-powerful "Leviathan", as Hobbes termed such a state), but rather a loosely formed, continually shifting pattern of conscious alliances.

Mutual aid

There are a number of things we might question about Stirner's vision. It's often seen as nihilistic and cynical, painting a bleak view of human nature. For Stirner, other people are merely a means to an end, and another person's value lies only in their usefulness: "For me you are nothing but – my food, even as I too am fed upon and turned to use

by you." However, in another sense, it's also a very idealistic view, in that it proposes that individuals can be conscious and principled enough to form his "union of egoists" – for, he does not deny, such alliances are necessary. We may, however, also question this view of human nature: isn't it true that human beings are naturally gregarious and community-minded, instinctively driven to form groups based on relationships and common interests? After all, your kids are related by blood, if nothing else, and there must be *some* bonds of mutual affection that stop them turning against one another *Lord of the Flies* style?

The Russian anarchist philosopher **Peter Kropotkin** (1842–1921) argued for just such a view. In line with the evolutionary theories of Charles Darwin (1809–82), Kropotkin agrees that nature involves the struggle among

> "We have only one relation to each other, that of usableness, of utility, of use."
> Max Stirner

species for limited resources; however, he also argued, *within* species, individuals cooperate for their "mutual aid" or benefit, and in fact that "Sociability is as much a law of nature as mutual struggle." Animals congregate in packs and herds, insects in colonies and hives, all to help their own species survive in the general struggle for resources and security. Such organization often involves naturally evolving differences in role, and mutual concern for welfare: prairie dogs will station sentries to keep lookout while their young play; elephants have been observed to show concern over their injured and grief over their deceased; even rats will look after those that have been wounded. Without denying the basic principles of Darwinism – the *natural selection* of "fitter" species over weaker ones, the merciless, instinct-driven battle for survival – Kropotkin argues that "altruism",

the apparently selfless concern of one being for another, is actually a vital survival strategy: "sociability is the greatest advantage in the struggle for life", while "unsociable species, on the contrary, are doomed to decay".

An anarchy of anarchies

While Stirner's outlook is individualist, Kropotkin's, like Marx's, is collectivist. However, like Stirner, Kropotkin rejects any overall authority (even a temporary one) that can guarantee private property or law, and rather trusts to what seem to be the natural tendencies of humans under certain conditions to voluntarily cooperate with one another, realizing that such strategies are necessary for survival. Kropotkin is generally considered an *anarcho-communist*, agreeing with Marx regarding the abolition of private property and wage-labour, resulting in a fair

society founded on mutual support. However, while both thinkers agreed regarding the end goal (more or less) – a classless, free and equal society – they differed in the means they thought should be employed. In line with his views on cooperation, Kropotkin thought that social equality should evolve from below, through a "horizontal" (non-hierarchical) network of voluntary local organizations. In contrast, Marx argued that, initially, a "workers' state" was needed to impose equality – a move that Kropotkin and other anarchists considered would lead to authoritarianism (which, in many cases, it did!).

As you might perhaps expect, there are various forms of anarchism. Anarchists are also sometimes referred to as *left-wing libertarians*, which can be confusing, as today the term "libertarian" often describes someone who believes in free-market economics and absence of state intervention – such as Robert Nozick (whom we'll consider later). However, "right-wing libertarians" such as

Basic philosophical question:

Does society need a centralized leadership or government, or can it be freer and fairer without one?

Nozick are not anarchists, but *minarchists*, who believe in minimal government (in your case, it would be the equivalent of asking your neighbour Mrs Grimthorpe to pop in daily to check on things). In contrast, while they differ in emphasis, what characterizes genuine anarchism is the lack of leadership and authority – the state – and its replacement by voluntary association and organization.

Making a decision:

Whether or not you can trust your kids to look after themselves (and your house) while you're away on holiday depends upon a number of factors. Whether or not they think of themselves as individuals or a collective, are they mature enough to recognize the need to cooperate for their mutual benefit? Or, freed from the authoritarian control of the State of Mum and Dad, are they more likely to engage in a pleasure-fuelled free-for-all of unlicensed self-indulgent abandon? With Kropotkin and Stirner, it all comes down to your view of human nature – or, perhaps, human nurture: how well have you brought them up?

Should I put my life on the internet?

Bentham • Foucault • Morozov • Huxley • Orwell • Postman

We are encouraged to share. "What's happening?" asks Twitter. "Write something..." suggests Facebook. We share pictures of our meals, our holiday snaps, recommend series for friends to watch on Netflix, and rate books for others to buy on Amazon. Our mobile phones track us, notifying friends that we're near – do we want to meet for coffee, perhaps? We live publicly, as if obeying a compulsion. It's almost as if an experience doesn't truly exist unless it is digitally memorialized and broadcast for all to see. Is that a problem?

While John Stuart Mill and John Locke worried about the potentially intrusive power of the state, the digital age has seen many of us seemingly surrender our privacy with gleeful abandon. During the Cold War, the Russian KGB and the East German Stasi would offer rewards for people to inform on one other; now, we freely inform on *ourselves*, willingly revealing our innermost thoughts and desires, personal tastes and favourite pastimes, with any comparative stranger. Of course, globally speaking, state oppression and censorship are not a thing of the past – there are still many countries where personal and political freedom are radically restricted – but, in Western democracies at least, the interconnectedness of modern technology has allowed the distinction between private and public to be significantly eroded.

Mass surveillance

This is not to say that today's security services are any less busy, of course. In fact, as recent events show, they may be busier than ever. In 2013 Edward Snowden, then working as an intelligence analyst for America's National Security Agency (NSA), began to feed information to various journalists concerning a mass surveillance project called PRISM, which basically granted the NSA access to the electronic activity of millions of people – private emails, phone calls, text messages. Perhaps most alarmingly (according to Snowden), this was not confined to "persons of interest", such as suspected terrorists or the intelligence agents of other countries ("spies"), but might involve everyone and anyone, regardless of status, nationality or political persuasion. All such data was to be "harvested" and collated, and, using advanced digital search techniques and ever-increasing computer power, sifted for things of interest, however that might be defined.

A similar issue exists with CCTV, which is an increasing presence in any modern town or city. You may argue that, being in a public place, you're not entitled to privacy, but with advances in face recognition software, such surveillance also provides the power to track you, to know where you are and where you've been. Isn't this (potentially) tantamount to stalking?

The common defence for such powers is, of course, the performance of the state's duty to prevent criminality and to keep us safe. And, of course, the *ability* to monitor is not the same as *actively* monitoring. But what effect does the fact that we *may* be under surveillance have upon freedom?

The Internet as Panopticon

The English utilitarian philosopher **Jeremy Bentham** created a plan for a modern prison, which he termed the Panopticon. This was a circular design, where all the prisoners' cells were open, facing a central watchtower. The idea was that, should they want to, the guards could look into any cell at any time. Of course, the idea was not for the guards to *actually* monitor all prisoners at all times. The guard tower should be so constructed that the guards were hidden, so no prisoner could ever tell if he were being watched. The result would be that the prisoners would behave *as if* they were being monitored; they would be, effectively, self-policing.

The French postmodernist philosopher **Michel Foucault** (1926–84) used Bentham's prison design as a metaphor for political power. The Panopticon does three things: it isolates prisoners, it makes them perpetually

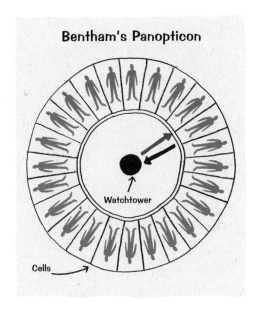

Bentham's Panopticon

Watchtower

Cells

visible, and it renders *actual* surveillance redundant (there need be no one in the watchtower). We might say the same about the internet and digital technology. Ironically, such power to connect isolates us – how often have you been in a room of people and everyone is silent, absorbed by their smartphones? It also gradually shapes how we think of ourselves, forcing us to create a distinct online identity. And, if Snowden is right, then we may be monitored at any time – even if it never actually happens – and so it also encourages us to moderate our behaviour: we self-police.

For Foucault, the Panopticon is a sort of template that shows how power works.

"Write something..."

Facebook

Traditionally, political power is seen as the ability to command obedience. However, Foucault argues, power is actually subtler than that. It shapes the way people *are* – their choices, how they think of themselves and how they behave. Is it really convenient that you express yourself in bursts of 140 characters or less? That you are contactable at any time or place by phone, email or text, or that your location can be tracked and monitored? We can try to opt out, of course – to switch off our phones, unplug our laptops, and so on. But as all aspects of society are shaped by technological developments – health and education, leisure and work – it seems an increasingly forlorn and futile gesture.

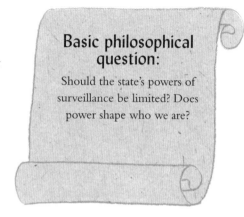

Basic philosophical question:

Should the state's powers of surveillance be limited? Does power shape who we are?

Dystopian visions

But isn't the internet also a force for political change? Didn't Facebook and Twitter help mobilize dissidents across the Middle East during the anti-government uprisings of the Arab Spring? Hasn't modern technology brought forth a new brand of activism, through WikiLeaks and the hacking group Anonymous, helping to hold corrupt powers accountable? The Belarusian writer **Evgeny Morozov** (b. 1984) agrees with Snowden that, while it has its benefits, the internet also empowers authoritarianism to better monitor its subjects. It's also far from clear that it will lead to greater political engagement – why not, as Morozov observes regarding his native Belarus, greater apathy and cynicism? In Belarus, he tells us, "no angry tweets or text messages, no matter how eloquent, have

been able to rekindle the democratic spirit of the masses, who, to a large extent, have drowned in a bottomless reservoir of spin and hedonism, created by a government that has read its Huxley". The reference to **Aldous Huxley** (1894–1963) here is to the English novelist's *Brave New World* (1932), a dystopic vision of a future where freedom is not ground out of us by an all-powerful, all-knowing repressive state (the "Big Brother" envisaged by **George Orwell**'s *Nineteen Eighty-Four*, 1949), but rather weakened by distraction – as **Neil Postman** (1931–2003) put it: "Orwell feared those who would

Foucault

"the major effect of the Panopticon: to induce in the inmate a state of conscious and permanent visibility that assures the automatic functioning of power."

1984

deprive us of information. Huxley feared those who would give us so much that we would be reduced to passivity and egoism. Orwell feared that the truth would be concealed from us. Huxley feared the truth would be drowned in a sea of irrelevance." Regardless of whether Orwell or Huxley's dystopias will ultimately win, Morozov is clear that the internet equally enables both. The belief that somehow the "Net" will free us all – what he calls "cyber-utopianism" – is therefore a delusion.

The end of privacy

As technology develops, it's likely that it will become more intimately woven into our lives. Soon, when the "Internet of Things" really takes off, it will be common for your fridge to text you when you're out of milk, or for your front door to tell you that you have mail (if, in fact, physical letters still exist). As this progress continues, the boundaries between private and public will continue to erode. In Dave Egger's novel *The Circle* (2013), a Google-like company wishes to usher in an age of "transparency", where everyone will wear a camera, publicly transmitting, 24/7, everything they see and do. As frightening as this feels to most of us, it does have a certain logic: if there were no privacy, there would be no crime or corruption; there'd be no loneliness, as people were forced to connect and share more, to empathize with others. Isn't that worth giving up your privacy for? No?

Making a decision:

Are you being watched? In light of recent revelations, it's safe to assume that the state has such capabilities, so it really depends how you feel about the state – you may think privacy's a reasonable price to pay to protect society. That aside, we might argue that your freedom already seems compromised. If Foucault is right, then the individual is not simply under the authority of the state, but exists within an interconnected web of ideas, attitudes and values of which "authority" is merely a part. Since technology is largely driven by commerce, you should also be mindful of whose agenda you're following. Do you share because you want to, or because Apple/Google/Facebook encourages you to? Do you want to live in a world of ever more targeted advertising, where corporations intrude even further into our private lives? Or, for the sake of greater convenience and ever more entertaining distractions, is that a price worth paying, too?

Can I trust the news?

Socrates • Plato • Protagoras • Gorgias • Chomsky • Herman

You've just read something on your Facebook timeline that outrages you. You're about to share it, but suddenly stop yourself: is it actually true? It may seem that there was once a time where "the news" was simply an account of current affairs, but more and more, through the rise of social media, we face sensationalist and dubiously sourced stories whose intention is not to inform us, but to manipulate our emotions and play on our prejudices. In this new world of "post-truth" and "alternative facts", of conspiracy theories and "fake news", how can we tell what's really true? But, actually, none of this is really new.

At his trial, the Greek philosopher **Socrates** (469–399 BCE), mentor to Plato, apologized to the jury that he hadn't prepared a polished speech in his defence, and that they should forgive him if he stumbled or paused in his answers. Such an apology seems odd to us today – surely truth matters more than style? But, as Neil Postman argues, for his Athenian audience the opposite was almost the case: it wasn't merely *what* was said that mattered, but *how* it was said. The study of speaking well was called *rhetoric*. Hearing this word, we now think of the figures of speech found in poetry, or the rabble-rousing speeches of politicians or hellfire preachers, but to the ancient Greeks it was much more. For them, goodness and beauty, truth and eloquence, were all aspects of the same thing: truth should also *look* good. Socrates

was famously ugly and unconventional and cared little for etiquette, so it's perhaps unsurprising that his peers found him guilty (of "corrupting the youth of Athens" and "refusing to recognize the gods"). Though most historians now consider the charges trumped-up, he *was* seeking to break away from traditions and ways of thinking that many of them were not yet ready to abandon.

Plato and the first "post-truthers"

Devastated by the death of his beloved teacher, **Plato** set about defending his reputation and continuing his struggle. Most of Plato's works take the form of "dialogues" – philosophical dramas, in many of which Socrates is the main character – and often his target is the very thing that

"Man is the measure of all things."
Protagoras

95

may have contributed to his mentor's downfall: the corruption of philosophy by rhetoric. The fault here, Plato thought, lay with the *sophists*, a breed of freelance tutors, specializing in the art of rhetoric. From this sprang a somewhat cynical and nihilistic philosophy. **Protagoras** (486–411 BCE), one of the first prominent sophists, famously declared that "Man is the measure of all things" – meaning, presumably, that there were no values or truths that existed independently of human subjectivity.

Protagoras' fellow sophist **Gorgias** (483–375 BCE) similarly declared that "Nothing exists", and that, even if something did, we couldn't know anything about it. Furthermore, on the off-chance that something *could* be known, we wouldn't be able to communicate it (I think that's called "hedging your bets"). The upshot of

all of this relativism and nihilism? Truth is what you can get away with. The sophists were therefore the first "post-truthers". Plato accordingly spends much of his philosophical career in attempting to establish that truth does exist, that it can be known, communicated and understood. But because truth can be hard to come by and difficult to understand, there's always scope for unscrupulous people to manufacture pleasing falsehoods and exploit convenient and lazy thinking.

From propaganda to fake news

Propaganda is, in modern times, often associated with totalitarian regimes: for example, the state control of the media by Joseph Goebbels (1897–1945), Hitler's Minister of Propaganda, tasked with spreading and justifying Nazi anti-Semitism; or *Pravda* (Russian for "truth"), the official newspaper of the Soviet Communist Party. But propaganda is actually any information used to promote a political or partisan cause. The Allies weren't shy in utilizing it during World War II, and it's estimated the US Air Force dropped around 6 billion pamphlets on the towns and cities of Germany and Japan – spreading disinformation, offering incentives to surrender, and undermining morale, among other purposes. The British even hatched a scheme to disseminate fake Nostradamus predictions, hoping that the known interest of some members of the German high command in the writings of the French astrologer would influence them to overthrow Hitler (see Ellic Howe's

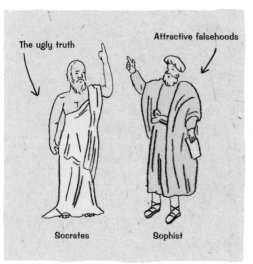

The ugly truth

Attractive falsehoods

Socrates

Sophist

Nostradamus and the Nazis, 1965). We may also talk of religious "propaganda" – where, in fact, the term originates, in reference to the part of the Catholic Church responsible for "spreading the faith" (in Latin, *propaganda fide*). The root connection here would therefore seem to be information that's intended to bypass or transcend reason: whether via prejudice, fear, faith or emotion.

In 2016 "post-truth" entered the *Oxford English Dictionary*, defined as "circumstances in which objective facts are less influential in shaping public opinion than appeals to emotion and personal belief" – and what is that if not propaganda by another name? The difference between traditional propaganda and modern "fake news" perhaps springs from the rise of the internet and social media and their greater power to influence. Obviously, the internet has had a positive effect, allowing access to a broader range of information and fact-checking resources. However, many political commentators now think it likely that the proliferation of false and misleading "news" articles may have played a large role in recent elections in France, the USA, the UK, and perhaps elsewhere. Facebook, Google and other vehicles for the spread

> ### Basic philosophical question:
> Does all news media involve a form of bias? What is the difference between news and propaganda?

of such stories have vowed to help fight this tide, but arguably they are themselves largely to blame. How many times have you "Googled" something and accepted the first answer, or not gone past the first page of results? And yet, the search results are "ranked" by Google; it is they that suggest their reliability and accuracy. Similarly, your Facebook feed is not simply a collection of things shared by your friends, but has been "edited" by Facebook's algorithm regarding what's popular or what it thinks you'll like. The massive potential for such services to filter and regulate what information we see is a worrying threat to the political process, not least of all because

"Post-truth (adj.): …relating to or denoting circumstances in which objective facts are less influential in shaping public opinion than appeals to emotion and personal belief."
Oxford English Dictionary

Propaganda Model

Raw news

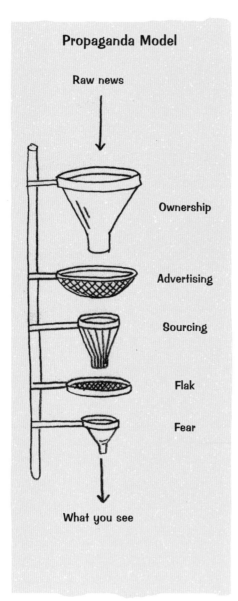

Ownership

Advertising

Sourcing

Flak

Fear

What you see

it can be "gamed" by those with extreme views or anti-democratic motives, or even antagonistic foreign states.

"Manufacturing consent"

But, once again, we should not allow recent events to lead us to assume that traditional or mainstream media are in some way above such conscious manipulation. In fact, it's common to think of newspapers and TV news as having some bias – left or right, populist or elitist. Generally, however, it's considered that such biases offset one another; while the editor of the *Washington Post* may have different views to that of the *Wall Street Journal*, their differences are the expression of freedom of speech, and so the media as a whole represent a spectrum of opinion, from which the reader may choose with whom to agree or disagree.

However, this traditional picture was questioned by **Noam Chomsky** and **Edward S Herman** (b. 1925) when they advanced what they called the "propaganda model" of the media. In it, they argued that the mainstream media were *not* in fact free, but rather promulgated the views of the Establishment (a country's political class, military, public organizations, dominant corporations and other vested interests). These all regulated the news more or less indirectly, using five filters: (1) *Ownership*: most news organizations are part of large corporations with specific business interests – truth comes second; (2) *Advertising*: advertisers can influence news by threatening to pull out; (3) *Sourcing*: government and other big organizations spin information, and can restrict access of "unfriendly" press to sources (important data, information on policies and programmes); (4) *Flak*: organizations can attack "negative" news through counter stories, political speeches, complaints, lawsuits and so on; and (5) *Fear*: danger from a real or imagined common enemy can be utilized to unify opinion through fear, and marginalize critics as unpatriotic.

So, while there might not be direct coercion or explicit censorship, news is nonetheless effectively *indirectly manufactured* through hitting the bottom line: profit. A newspaper that loses advertisers, suffers restricted access to sources, is subject to lawsuits and so on will risk loss of sales and revenue. If true, Chomsky and Herman supply a damning critique of political democracy: what appears to be disagreement between different elements in media and politics is actually just cosmetic or trivial: about the important issues (business, war, taxation), whatever the party or paper, the Establishment is united.

Making a decision:

The difference between news and propaganda is not so clear as we might hope. However, while sceptics, sophists and postmodernists question the existence or value of truth, we can admit that all viewpoints carry bias without going that far. We must develop techniques for analysing news stories – where they come from, whether the story appears "offline" anywhere, how balanced and well written it is – and so on. But if all mainstream media are propagandist (to some extent), how can we check it against itself? Well, as Chomsky responds, since individuals write news, you can still find truthful, relatively unbiased reporting, even in the broadly propagandist mainstream media – you just have to look.

My teenage son calls me a "fascist" – am I?

Plato • Popper • Arendt • Hobbes • Marx • Machiavelli • Rousseau • Raz

He wants to go to a party; you think he should study for his upcoming exams. Tempers fray, voices are raised. Before it gets out of hand, you lay down the law – "You're not going out, and that's final!" – provoking a string of uncomplimentary epithets suggesting that your politics are somewhat to the right of Mussolini's. But you've got his best interests at heart! Isn't it your parental duty to enforce those? Even if it makes you seem a little...well...totalitarian?

You wouldn't be the first dictator to justify his actions this way. In criticizing **Plato**'s *Republic*, the Austrian philosopher **Karl Popper** argued that "our greatest troubles spring from something that is as admirable and sound as it is dangerous – from our impatience to better the lot of our fellows". Plato's *genuine concern* for others ironically led him to create a rigid, authoritarian state, for too much freedom provides too much room for error. But isn't the nature of freedom that we can make our own mistakes? Isn't it better to be free and occasionally "mistaken" than unfree and "correct"? And who defines "correct"?

But, for all Popper's criticisms, Plato *was* keen to distinguish legitimate authority from tyranny, the worst form of government, where power resided with a single (usually self-seeking) individual. Authority isn't just the capacity to make someone do what you want – you can have authority without power (your son can sneak out against your wishes), and power without authority (you could illegally lock him in his room). So when he calls you a "fascist", is he implying your "rule" is illegitimate, overly authoritarian or simply unjust? Or all of these?

So what does "fascism" mean?

"Fascist" is now generally a term of disapproval. Historically, the term can be traced back to ancient Rome, where the *fasces*, a bundle of sticks tied around an axe, denoted a magistrate's power and authority. Symbolically, it also suggests

> *"What a monument of human smallness is this idea of the philosopher king."*
> Karl Popper

"strength through unity": one stick can be easily broken; many cannot. Various political movements have termed themselves "fascist", or had the term applied to them, but a few – Mussolini's *Fasci*, Hitler's Nazis – have deliberately echoed the patriotic, warlike and absolutist attitudes of ancient Imperial Rome. Modern fascists have therefore opposed liberalism and democracy, promoted fervent nationalism, favoured centralized control (an individual dictator or military junta) and state economic regulation, and justified violence as a political tool.

Interestingly, communist regimes (traditionally considered *left-wing*), although often contrasted with fascist (*right-wing*) governments, share a number of these features. This perhaps suggests that the traditional left/right distinction is too simplistic, for – aside from the fact that many modern Marxists would consider Stalinist Russia (for example) as not genuinely communist – such regimes are equally *totalitarian* (the state intimately interferes in its subjects' lives), and *collectivist* (nationhood is more important than individuality). They do differ in some respects: communism is internationalist, fascism is nationalistic; communism is atheist, fascism favours religious uniformity; communism advocates a classless society with communal ownership, fascism allows limited private ownership within a rigid, hierarchical society. But in practice it's easy to see how the effects of both communism and fascism

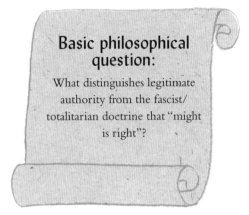

Basic philosophical question:

What distinguishes legitimate authority from the fascist/totalitarian doctrine that "might is right"?

were largely identical: the liberal, individual freedoms celebrated by democratic societies all but disappeared.

"Might is right"

The common roots of Stalinism and Nazism were noted by the German philosopher **Hannah Arendt** (1906–75), who argued that such forms of government were new, for they tried to silence not only critics and political opponents, but the population in general. Under totalitarianism, even a regime's supporters therefore effectively gave up their political rights and freedoms in exchange for a unified society of narrow traditions and values. This might comfort some (e.g. conservative "Aryan" Germans), but the rest suffered suppression of individuality, persecution, terror and possibly death.

Assuming you resist the temptation to point a webcam at your son's window in case he tries to sneak out, closely monitor and restrict his internet activity, or try

What makes authority legitimate? This question affects all authority figures - from political leaders to parents and teachers.

to read his phone messages, you can justly claim your rule is not totalitarian. Fascism is also often associated with the justification that "might is right"; that, simply by virtue of having power, a government claims authority. **Thomas Hobbes** similarly justified the rulership of his all-powerful sovereign (*see* page 82). Even **Karl Marx** thought that communism could only be established through "revolutionary terror" emerging amid "the murderous death agonies of the old society and the bloody birth throes of the new". And **Niccolò Machiavelli**, of course, in advocating the approach that now bears his name, justified almost any methods in maintaining rule (*see* page 14).

Realpolitik

The "Machiavellian" nature of modern politics, where states standardly adopt a realpolitik attitude (where ideology comes second to practical considerations), suggests that many still consider that ends justify means. If grounding him, or bugging his phone, were the surest way to serve your son's best interests, why shouldn't you? As **Jean-Jacques Rousseau** argued, sometimes, when people foolishly fail to grasp what is right – the ideal wisdom of the state's "General Will", as he called it – authority may step in to ensure that they are "forced to be free". If your son were rational, he'd freely choose to study rather than party, surely? Only peer pressure and juvenile impulse gratification steer him awry. Better, then, that you choose for him.

It's no coincidence, perhaps, that the adherents of Marx and Rousseau respectively perpetrated bloody terrors in the name of their causes. Once we abandon the idea that the right course of action is to be decided by an open, democratic process, then abuses seem inevitable. But even democratic societies face the question of justification. What, then, can you appeal to in order to make your son see sense (if, in fact, that's what it is)? Some form of social contract? But, as we've seen (and your clever son has read Hume!), he's never signed anything, and it's not like he can opt out – should he prefer homelessness to the gulag you call his home?

Knowing better

One answer you might appeal to is the Normal Justification Theory proposed by **Joseph Raz**. The best way to think of legitimate authority, Raz argues, is as helping ensure that subjects comply with things they already have reason to do. In other words, your son (presumably) wants to pass his exams; all you're doing is trying to ensure this. That is, you only "know better" because you have a better grasp of what's required if he wants to achieve his goals: he thinks he can party and pass; you know (from your own sorry experience, perhaps) that he can't. Does that make you a fascist? No. A paternalist? Maybe. You are his parent, after all.

Making a decision:

Parental authority, like state authority, is difficult to rationally justify. Some parents merely assume not only that they know best, but that this entitles them to enforce whatever rules they see fit (authoritarianism). However, when and where possible, it's arguably better to try to win over your son by rational means: your rules and authority are merely ways to help him achieve what he really wants. Of course, to do so, you should also be open to questioning: are you imposing what's best for him, or what you want?

My new department miss their old boss. Should I just sack everyone?

Burke • Machiavelli

Your new job as head of department looks like it will be a challenge. To be frank, things are a mess – inefficient, bureaucratic, even a bit corrupt. The old boss was head for 20 years and left a very established way of doing things. Since many of those left are loyal to the old ways, would it be simplest to start again from scratch? Sack everyone and let them reapply for their jobs?

Your dilemma is a common one in business, as well as for football managers and even step- and foster parents. It is also, of course, a common political problem. The old leader steps down, but all her old cronies are safely entrenched. If you try to quietly dispose of them, they may kick up a fuss or start a rebellion; if you leave them in place, they may block changes or even sow discord. Advocates of radical change or even violent revolution therefore justify such approaches with the need to start with a clean slate: if you don't sweep away the old, corrupt order, how can a new, just one replace it? The problem with such an approach, of course, is that you throw away the baby with the bathwater; all that was valuable about the old regime – its established methods, its institutions, the accrued wisdom of its civil servants – will disappear also.

I'm really looking forward to working with you

"A new broom sweeps clean."
Traditional

"one should wish to be both, but, because it is difficult to unite them in one person, it is much safer to be feared than loved"

Machiavelli

Gradual and orderly change

It was such concerns that convinced the Irish political philosopher **Edmund Burke** (1729–97) that all political and social change should be constitutional, gradual and orderly, with due respect for established tradition. While he did not oppose the idea of revolution in principle – he supported American independence – in his *Reflections on the Revolution in France* (1790) Burke rejected what he saw as the Jacobins' brutal and reckless overthrow of tradition in the name of "reason" and "progress". Society, he argued, is like a body, made up of various parts that serve the whole. As such, while change constantly takes place, the system as a whole is maintained. To update his analogy a little, cells die off and are replaced, the body grows and changes gradually, but the overall organization suffers no radical change. Thus, "by preserving the method of nature in the conduct of the state, in what we improve we are never wholly new; in what we retain we are never wholly obsolete".

Burke is a fascinating mix of radical, liberal and reactionary ideas – some have even claimed him as a forerunner of anarchism! – but his general approach is conservative: we should "conserve" what is good about society, while allowing means for it to improve itself. Burke is therefore, in many ways, an anti-Enlightenment figure: what is "good" might seem "irrational" at times (the old boss's tradition of allowing half-hour coffee breaks arguably eats into productivity), but such "prejudices" (as Burke calls them) may play a positive role (fostering team

> ## Basic philosophical question:
> Can meaningful political change be accomplished only through revolution?

spirit). Applied to the later revolution in Russia, we can see that, in vindication of his conservative views, he would oppose the idea of rational progress that the revolution sought to embody, and point to the social disruption, terror and human tragedy that it caused. Stalin's economic policies caused famine and death on a huge scale, and, when World War II broke out, his paranoid purge of the old guard of army and navy generals severely reduced Soviet military competence. Change is not always good.

Keeping what's good

Niccolò Machiavelli took a similar position, arguing that it is easier for a new ruler to hold a "hereditary" state (one where its people are "long accustomed to the family of their prince") than a newly established domain. In taking over the reins, it is therefore "sufficient only not to transgress the customs of [the old ruler's] ancestors". In other words, if you don't rock the boat too much, no one will challenge you once

> *"[The Prince] who has annexed them…has only to bear in mind two considerations: the one, that the family of their former lord is extinguished; the other, that neither their laws nor their taxes are altered, so that in a very short time they will become entirely one body with the old principality."*
> Niccolò Machiavelli

they realize that things will carry on much as before. Assuming, of course, that you have taken precautions to ensure that "the family of their former lord is extinguished" (we don't want the old boss's second-in-command sabotaging you so she can get your job now, do we?).

But what if the old customs are precisely the problem? If you have to make unpopular changes, Machiavelli says, then it's best to do it quickly and all in one go – then preferably to blame someone else! So, you might sack some prominent members of the old guard, but blame it on budget cuts or a decision made higher up the chain of command. Some such forthright action early on sends a message to the others that you are not to be trifled with, but, as long as this is followed by signs that you are also reasonable and respect what is good about the "old ways" (e.g. coffee breaks), then the remaining employees will eventually respond positively. After all, most people just want a wage, at the end of the day, don't they?

Making a decision:

Whether in politics or business, change is easier when people are on your side. This either means, as Machiavelli points out, that they respect your authority, or that they are confident that they will continue to benefit as members of the new order. As Burke points out, any radical upheaval is also likely to risk losing what was good about the old order, and to cause disruption and turmoil. However, a general degree of flexibility and openness to change is healthy.

Should I go to jail for some trees?

Thoreau • Gandhi • Luther King • Rawls • Banksy • Tejaratchi

There's a beautiful patch of woodland where you used to play as a child. It's the only green space for miles around, its ancient trees providing a rare oasis for wildlife in the ever-spreading urban jungle. However, local authorities have just agreed to sell the land to real-estate developers, to be bulldozed for luxury apartments. All legal means to block it have been exhausted. What options are left? Lie down before the bulldozers? Chain yourself to a tree?

While civil disobedience has existed in various forms for centuries, and has been defined in various ways, the term itself originates with the American transcendentalist philosopher **Henry David Thoreau** (1817–62). Displeased with the American government's ongoing sanction of slavery and its participation in the Mexican–American War (1846–8), Thoreau advocated active resistance. Where government is unjust, the citizen's first duty is not to the law, but to his own conscience. Therefore, we're entitled to actively withhold our consent – such as through the non-payment of taxes – in order to pressure government to change its policies.

Winning hearts and minds

Civil disobedience is different from legal protest. Given that the land has already been sold, it's probably illegal for you to interfere with redevelopment, and to do so would put you at the risk of prosecution. But if you're prepared to face arrest, lying in front of a tractor will have more effect than holding placards while trees are felled. The Indian civil rights campaigner

Mohandas Gandhi (1869–1948) used mass non-violent protest to pressure the British Empire for Indian independence. In the USA, **Martin Luther King Jr.** (1929–68) employed similar methods to protest against various forms of racial injustice. Both religious pacifists were influenced by Thoreau, and their actions emphasized the importance of non-violent actions. As Gandhi observed, "Victory attained by violence is tantamount to a defeat, for it is momentary." In protesting against war, oppression and injustice, both the ends and the means must reflect one another: the point is to win hearts and minds.

But you're not seeking world peace, just to save your local woodland. In the 19th-century, Luddites protested against the effects of industrialization upon skilled trade and wages by destroying machines. Could you tamper with the tractors or sabotage the chainsaws? But there are always more tractors and chainsaws, and damage to property will likely prejudice your cause and alienate sympathy. So, if you can create maximum publicity whilst appearing rational and principled, then the more the

developers will feel public pressure – no company wants to receive bad press.

So, you've decided that your protest should be non-violent but, to be most effective, also requires illegal disruption (sit-ins and other forms of "passive resistance"). What happens next? Well, the developers call the police, who arrest you and forcibly drag you away. Would that be worth it? All for some trees?

In *A Theory of Justice* (1971), **John Rawls** argued that facing the consequences of your illegal protest was an essential requirement for civil disobedience – otherwise, how is it different from criminality? Allowing yourself to be arrested shows not only that your actions are principled, but also that – in all other respects – you respect the rule of law. You're not a lawless anarchist (in

"The only obligation which I have a right to assume is to do at any time what I think right."
Henry Thoreau

the common sense), but a citizen seeking political change through principled, rational (if illegal) means.

Rewriting the rules

However, while principled, it's potentially ineffective: your woodland may still be razed. Rawls's approach also arguably discourages activism: few will risk prison, and it asks a lot of individuals to go against companies and governments that possess far greater resources than they (to manipulate the media, hire fancy high-powered lawyers or even – depending on how unscrupulous they are – retaliate by targeting identifiable ringleaders). Such powers may seek to

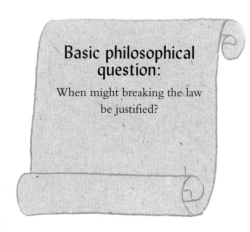

Basic philosophical question:

When might breaking the law be justified?

gag whistle-blowers, even where leaking information might be considered in the public interest. If you could illicitly share

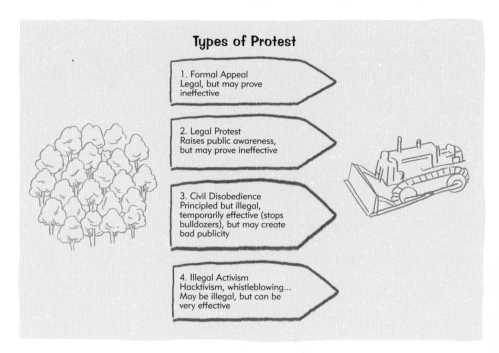

Types of Protest

1. Formal Appeal
Legal, but may prove ineffective

2. Legal Protest
Raises public awareness, but may prove ineffective

3. Civil Disobedience
Principled but illegal, temporarily effective (stops bulldozers), but may create bad publicity

4. Illegal Activism
Hacktivism, whistleblowing... May be illegal, but can be very effective

> *"Any advert in a public space that gives you no choice whether you see it or not is yours. It's yours to take, re-arrange and re-use."*
> Sean Tejaratchi

information that revealed the developers had bribed the authorities, would you do so, at the risk that your criminal activity might be revealed?

Such imbalance in power explains the Occupy movement, WikiLeaks and the internet hacker group Anonymous, whose actions suggest the best strategy is not public, principled, civil disobedience by identifiable individuals, but methods that allow for potential anonymity; for protestors to protect themselves from reprisal by hiding their identity behind a mask; for computer hackers to anonymously disseminate illicitly gained sensitive information or bring down corporate websites; even, under cover of night, for graffiti artists to mock, deface or "hack" corporate ads and billboards. As UK street artist **Banksy** (identity unknown) has argued – borrowing from graphic designer **Sean Tejaratchi** (b. *c.*1970) – such subterfuge is justified by the constant intrusion of corporate and government power into personal life. For Banksy, any media in the public space, which you are unable to avoid, is "yours to take, re-arrange and re-use. You can do whatever you like with it. Asking for permission is like asking to keep a rock someone just threw at your head" (*Cut It Out*, 2004). When power and money rewrite the rules, why should you continue to play by them?

Making a decision:

Whatever methods you choose, there's a long tradition of civil disobedience that you can appeal to for justification – not to save you from prosecution, but at least to make your stand respectable and principled (whether it will be effective is another matter). Modern approaches reveal frustration at the relative powerlessness of the individual. Does this justify a resort to subterfuge? Whatever you decide, you should probably be prepared to accept the consequences.

Should I get married?

Aristotle • Plato • Aquinas • Rousseau • Kant • Marx • Freud

Fed up with corruption, scandal and ineptitude, you've decided to enter politics – I mean, surely you can't do a *worse* job? However, as you discuss the matter with friends and advisers, a few point out that it might be a good move for you to get married. To become a politician?! But marriage vows haven't kept the holders of the highest offices in the land from infidelity! And you've been with your partner for many years now; you're both happy, and have never felt the need to tie the knot – so why now? Just to reassure the electorate that you're "respectable"?

While you might think such things a private matter, a surprising number of philosophers have emphasized the importance of the "nuclear family" in providing the basis for social order. In fact, for **Aristotle**, the family was "the association established by nature for the supply of men's everyday wants", where man commanded and woman obeyed. Early societies were an extension of this – not that the organization of the state should *reflect* that of the family – a man might be "king" in his own home, but the state need not be a monarchy. Nonetheless, the family provided the building block of society, fostering the bonds of natural attraction between men and women required to procreate and raise children.

The perfect marriage

In this, Aristotle rejected the more radical view of his mentor **Plato**, who, in his *Republic*, saw in the family an obstacle to justice, fostering private interests over public ones. By making marriages temporary, state-arranged couplings merely for the production of children, and by making the whole community of guardians responsible for their communal upbringing, Plato sought to use sexual attraction as a cement for society as a whole. However, in a later work, *The Laws*, he allowed a more conventional picture of marriage, and is even responsible, in his *Symposium*, for giving us the idea of "soul mates" (put into the mouth of the playwright Aristophanes). So, his overall message is somewhat mixed.

The Christian Church used Aristotle's arguments to promote its own ideal of monogamy, and such thinkers as the Italian priest and friar **Thomas Aquinas** (1225–74) even considered it an expression of "natural law", where woman – though, as Aristotle put it "defective and misbegotten" – is nonetheless ideally equipped to be "a helper in the work of generation", whereas man is "yet further ordered to a still nobler vital action, and that is intellectual operation". In other words, marriage is handy for rearing children, and monogamy provides the one justifiable outlet for the irrational sexual impulse, leaving men free to develop their higher selves.

And do you agree to take mutual possession of each other's sexual attributes so long as you both shall live?

judgment of father and husband as that of the church" (*Emile*, 1762).

Immanuel Kant saw marriage as a contract, involving "the union of two people of different sexes with a view to the mutual possession of each other's sexual attributes for the duration of their lives" (*Metaphysics of Morals*, 1797), a turn of phrase not likely to spur a rush to the altar or registry office. Like Christian theologians, Kant seems preoccupied with making sex respectable by allotting it the sole purpose of procreation. Other than that, he observes that marriage involves each party treating the other as if they were material possessions – as objects, or means to an end. Normally, in Kant's philosophy, this would be a problem: it is treating others as means to our own ends, not as ends in themselves, that results in immorality. However, because such "possession" is mutual, this objectification is in this instance justified; you get me, but I get you back – as long as neither of us breaks the contract!

Similarly, **Jean-Jacques Rousseau** defines woman's primary role in marriage as serving her husband, bearing and rearing his children. Unlike sons, whose education Rousseau has lots to say about, a daughter's education consists in knowing her place; she will believe what she's told. For instance, in matters of religion, "Unable to judge for themselves [females] should accept the

Marx on marriage

I have covered the feminist criticism of patriarchal society elsewhere (*see* page 63), but it is still quite startling from a modern perspective to note how many of the great (male) philosophers have shared similarly

"Love is born into every human being; it calls back the halves of our original nature together; it tries to make one out of two and heal the wound of human nature."
Plato

conservative, husband-centric views on marriage and family. However, marriage and family do not escape **Karl Marx's** economic critique, where he considers them an expression of the same attitudes as relate to property: men controlled, possessed and exploited women and biological production much as capitalists did the workers and the means of economic production, helping to generate wealth that could be passed on to male heirs (it's easy to see how Marx's views have influenced feminism) – but what then did he propose in its place?

Much as property should be "liberated" and shared communally, so Marx thought the family should be "abolished", and people left to form free associations. In other words, family was a form of oppression, a relationship of controller and controlled. However, once the restrictions relating to marriage and family were done away with,

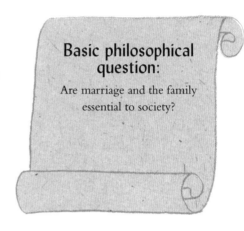

Basic philosophical question:

Are marriage and the family essential to society?

then people might be free to develop their own forms of relationship, monogamous or otherwise. We could spend much time trying to work out the pros and cons, and the practicalities of Marxist "free love" – and many have – but his main objective is to unmask the lie that any deviation from

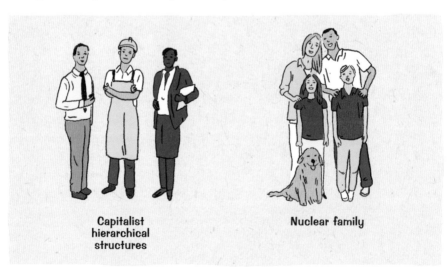

Capitalist hierarchical structures

Nuclear family

the norm of the nuclear family is in some way "immoral", for what is actually at stake, he says, is not "morality", but economics – *ownership and control*.

The Austrian psychologist **Sigmund Freud** (1856–1939) agreed, casting doubts on the biological and psychological fitness of human beings for lifelong monogamy, which, he argued, frequently resulted in misery – infidelity and hypocrisy, or else neurosis.

An institution in decline?

The last 50 years or so have seen a gradual but steady fall in marriage rates in many liberal democracies, coinciding with (depending on denomination) the general decline in religious belief and the relaxation of divorce laws. However, more recently, changes to laws and attitudes relating to same-sex marriage have seen many homosexual couples embrace marriage, finally achieving a parity with heterosexuals long denied them. Aside from an expression of personal commitment, at stake here are the sort of entitlements that early feminists fought for: concerning property, income, parental rights. Before we dismiss marriage and family completely as an outmoded form of social and political control, it's likely that, even in secular societies, such structures will remain – albeit in revised, liberal form – both as a means of expressing personal obligation (to partners and children), and to ensure certain legal obligations and rights. Perhaps, in this at least, Aristotle and his followers were right, and Marx too idealistic: for society as a whole to function, individuals must build bonds of affection and recognize moral and legal obligations to one another – whatever form that takes.

Making a decision:

While marriage and family may never go completely out of fashion, it seems that the nature of these is changing, along with – in some societies, at least – a greater acceptance of different ways of life and sexual attitudes. Wherever you live, you will therefore likely feel less pressure to get married than you might have in previous generations. Many societies now also protect the rights of couples who have lived together as if married (a definition that is gradually broadening). Assuming you agree with these changes, and feel your status and rights adequately protected where you live, then, rather than bowing to the pressure of "tradition", whether you're a politician in the public eye or not, the primary reason for you to marry would seem to be personal.

Rights

Chapter 4

My plane has crashed on a desert island. How will I and the other surviving passengers get along until we are rescued?

Locke • Bentham • Plato • Hart

It's your worst nightmare. On your way to a Tahitian holiday, your plane has a catastrophic engine failure and crashes into the Pacific Ocean. Luckily, you and your family survive, as do a number of the other passengers, and together you are washed up on the nearest landmass, an isolated, uninhabited island. As the days pass, and you wait to be rescued, it gradually dawns on you that you may be there for some time. You have some supplies (flotsam from the crash) and some natural resources (fresh water, shade and some weird-looking but potentially edible pig-like creatures). So, you have fair odds of survival – as long as you organize yourselves and agree some basic rules.

But problems have already started to crop up. A vegetarian passenger argues that a large share of the plane's surviving ready meals (which are mostly vegetarian) should be his, because he can't eat wild pig or fish, and there appear to be no edible fruits. He also won't help to hunt. Someone else insists that passengers should all help to build a place of worship, which will not only be time-consuming and energy-sapping, but will use up some of the island's limited natural resources – wouldn't it be higher priority to build a shelter? You voice your concerns, but another passenger – a lawyer – points out that you may be castaways, but you are not uncivilized beasts; you all naturally possess fundamental basic human rights, the observance of which are just as important as

survival. A bit dramatic, you think (obviously a trial lawyer), but is she right? I mean, there aren't any public institutions around to ensure such rights, no law courts for your bombastic friend to enforce them in (not yet, anyway…). Shouldn't you all simply do whatever is needed to survive, even if that involves compromising some social and cultural privileges?

Locke vs. Bentham

As we've seen, **John Locke** thought rights "self-evident" to reason, while **Jeremy Bentham** thought them "nonsense on stilts" (*see* page 58) – but what *are* rights? You may consider yourself as having the right to freedom of speech and expression, to property, not to eat pigs, or to practise freedom of

Bentham
Legal rights

VS.

Locke
Natural rights

religion, but what gives you those rights? Are such rights in some way "inalienable" (you will possess them no matter what, even on a desert island)? Are you born with them? Or do they require government and society to grant and ensure them?

Bentham attacked the idea of "natural rights" not because he thought that citizens should not possess *any* rights, but merely because he thought that only the law could provide them. If we consider rights to be "natural", he argued – that we possess the right to freedom of speech simply by virtue of our natural ability to think and

communicate – then that would seem to grant us the "right" to say *anything*. But surely this right would be too broad: what about situations where speaking our minds might get us into trouble, or cause "harm" to others? Yet if such rights *are* inherent, then any limiting legislation seems like a form of oppression. So, the idea of natural rights makes no sense, because rights can exist *only* within a legal framework, granted and ensured by society (a view known as *legal positivism*). In relation to your desert island, Bentham would argue not only that you needn't be bound by the laws from the

"These rights are liberty, property,
safety and resistance to oppression."
Declaration of the Rights of Man and of the Citizen

119

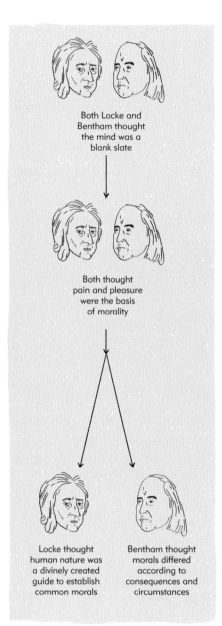

Both Locke and
Bentham thought
the mind was a
blank slate

Both thought
pain and pleasure
were the basis
of morality

Locke thought
human nature was
a divinely created
guide to establish
common morals

Bentham thought
morals differed
according to
consequences and
circumstances

society you have separately been brought up in, but also that any rights granted would need to be relative – that is, balanced with the greater concern for the community's survival.

While Bentham makes some telling points here, the flip side of this argument raises equally important concerns. Locke's purpose in considering certain rights "natural" was so that there *could be* no situation in which they were suppressed. Thus, the Locke-inspired *Declaration of the Rights of Man and of the Citizen* (1789), a key document in the French Revolution, considered "liberty, property, safety and resistance against oppression" to be *universal* rights, in that they applied everywhere, to all people, and at all times. If such rights were merely legal (granted by the state), then there might come a time, place or particular set of circumstances in which the state revoked them or considered them not to apply. The work of human rights organizations such as Amnesty International therefore would seem to rely on the assumption, embodied in the *Universal Declaration of Human Rights* adopted by the United Nations in 1948, that rights can be protected only if they are considered inalienable, and not therefore subject to change or amendment, the greed of corporations or the whim of dictators. According to this view, on Weird Pig Island (as I've decided to call it), vegetarianism and freedom of worship will therefore be guaranteed and protected as fundamental human rights.

> *"I doubt not, but from self-evident Propositions, by necessary Consequences, as incontestable as those in Mathematics, the measures of right and wrong might be made out."*
> John Locke

The nature of morality

Underlying this conflict are two slightly differing views regarding the nature of morality. To begin with, both Locke and Bentham agree that experience is the basis of knowledge – they are both empiricists. As such, the basis of moral knowledge is experience: we *evolve* conceptions of good/bad based on what is pleasurable/painful (a view known as *philosophical hedonism*). However, unlike Bentham, Locke argues that there is a "higher" or "true" good that human beings can eventually reason toward. In this sense, Locke sees moral philosophy as on a par with geometry or some other deductive science. He argues that, while our senses play a key role, we develop our views of right and wrong by reasoning about our experiences. I might get pleasure from stealing, but eventually – through considering the pain of punishment, or being stolen from – realize that a better course of action is to respect one another's rights to property. For Locke, there is only one way this can work out: each rational person will eventually deduce, through reasoning about experience, the same set of "natural rights".

But is this likely? Unlike **Plato**, who thought that our ideas of right and wrong exist separately from experience, implanted in our minds before birth (what he called the *forms*), Locke thought the mind a "blank slate", waiting to be written on by experience. But won't experiences "write on" each person differently? Just as I like the taste of strong cheese and you don't, or you like mountain climbing and it gives me vertigo, won't our views about theft, or torture, or freedom of speech similarly differ? While he's not completely clear, Locke seems to want to say that pain and pleasure are placed in us by God as guides to moral knowledge. But even if this were true, won't *different* associations relating to pain and pleasure simply lead us to evolve different moralities? This would lead to moral relativism: the belief that there is no single standard of truth to judge moral rights by. If true, then we can't have natural rights, because naturally, we evolve differently – which is, of course, what led Bentham to his version of utilitarianism: we can't judge morality by some absolute standard, but

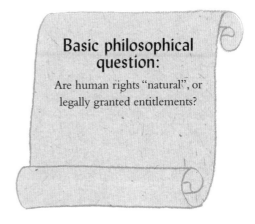

Basic philosophical question:

Are human rights "natural", or legally granted entitlements?

only by its consequences, of whether it causes more pleasure (or less pain) for the majority.

Another perspective

As we've seen, one of the criticisms of utilitarianism is that, under certain circumstances, it can seem to justify what would traditionally be seen as *immoral* acts. According to Bentham's utilitarianism, if selective theft and murder result in more overall "happiness", then that's the "right" thing to do. If Weird Pig Island were run on utilitarian grounds, then we might find that majority rule would result in the oppression of certain rights. Does that mean then that there can be no "universal" and "inalienable" rights? Not necessarily.

Locke's justification for natural rights seems slightly confused – perhaps one reason why he is not best known for his moral philosophy – but it is only one possible approach, and there are others. Another, though partial, defence of the view of rights as a natural entitlement has been proposed by British legal philosopher **H L A Hart** (1907–92). All moral rights limit freedom, in some way: having the right to own property means that no one else has the right to *your* property. How are we justified in limiting each other's freedom in this way? The question only makes sense if we assume that, prior to any agreements or legislation, people equally possess the general natural right to be free. In other words, the mere fact that we seek a reason or justification for limiting a person's freedom implies that he or she *already* possesses a *natural right* to freedom. Otherwise, why would we seek a justification? However, Hart's argument would still only prove that we have a *general* right to be free; even if we possess it, we still need legally enforced rights for other things.

Making a decision:

As we'll see, there are other bases for considering certain human rights universal and inalienable, but basing the constitution of Weird Pig Island on the assumption that we all possess certain "natural rights" would be, at best, controversial, for – as with many other specific rights – it's not clear that either vegetarianism or freedom of worship are directly justifiable by appeal to features universally possessed by human beings, whose views on such things differ.

I've just seen a UFO! Why is the government lying to us?

Kant • Plato • Bentham • Dworkin • Nagel

It's a clear night, and you're walking home from your local watering hole. You glance up, and suddenly notice a strange light. It bobs about for a bit, reverses direction, then suddenly shoots vertically into the night sky with immense velocity. What on earth was that? You inform the local paper, which politely enquires as to how much, exactly, you had to drink. Unabashed, you take it to your local politician, who assures you that, *if* UFOs existed, then the government would tell us; they haven't, so they don't. But you know what you saw! The government is lying! What can you do?

Governments often justify keeping secrets by appealing to national security, or the public interest. *If* aliens existed, then it would cause national panic for us to find out; better, then, to gradually accustom the public to the idea – by sowing truths through Hollywood blockbusters, sci-fi novels and half-jokey references in popular culture (at least, that's how *I'd* do it…). If you're not a believer, you can of course substitute any other number of more terrestrial examples – under-the-counter foreign arms sales, the extent of electronic surveillance of the public, or "covert action" in foreign countries. Who are *they* to keep secrets from *us*? As citizens, don't we have a *right* to know the truth?

Categorical imperatives

A popular basis for human rights is that provided by the moral philosophy of **Immanuel Kant**, and it is one where the importance of truth-telling plays a central role. It is a human being's possession of

reason, Kant argued, that both imposes duties and grants rights. Because we are, perhaps, the only beings that can choose our own rational *ends* (or goals), it would be immoral for one person to act in a way that stopped another from achieving those goals (presuming them to be legitimate). In Kant's eyes, the liar's *illegitimate* actions therefore frustrate your *legitimate* desire to know the truth.

But what makes an action "legitimate" or "illegitimate" in the first place? It's not so much that such deceit contravenes our "natural right" not to be lied to, but rather that the actions themselves involve a sort of rational contradiction. If everyone lied, then there would be no such things as deals, promises or contracts – no moral or legal obligations at all. Society itself would fall apart. But Kant is not here appealing to the consequence of your actions (as a utilitarian would), but rather trying to show how immorality is incoherent. You can't justify thieving or lying, or any other immoral action, any more than you can make sense of round squares or straight curves. A world in which it's OK to break a promise is one where promises cease to exist.

According to Kant, moral laws must be universalizable: "Inexperienced in the course of world affairs and incapable of being prepared for all the changes that happen in it, I ask myself only 'Can you also will that your maxim should become a universal law?'." This rule is known as the *categorical imperative*. An *imperative* is a command to do something ("Tell me about UFOs"); a *hypothetical* imperative would be a command you must follow *if* you wanted to achieve something ("If you want me to vote for you, tell me the truth about UFOs"); but a *categorical* imperative is a command that you *must* do, no matter what ("You must tell me the truth about UFOs"). To be moral is therefore to follow those rules that apply in all circumstances. The government should tell us the truth not because it will benefit itself in some way or serve some purpose, but just because *it's the right thing to do*. So, even if it's for our own good, a lie is *always* wrong, because – for both liar and lied-to – it harms our human dignity and frustrates our ability to achieve our rational goals.

Simple imperative

Hypothetical imperative

Categorical imperative

Noble lies

In practical political terms, however, Kant's approach would seem to be disastrous. There are numerous situations where governments might justifiably conceal the truth – prior to frustrating some criminal enterprise or terrorist plot, for example. Kant would say that this needn't involve lying, of course –

"Act only on that maxim through which you can at the same time will that it should become a universal law."
Immanuel Kant

a government could simply say, "We cannot talk about that" – but in many situations this would be tantamount to an admission. "Does the government have evidence of UFOs, Mr President?" "I'm sorry, I can't confirm or deny that." (and the journalists scramble over one another to break the news…). Some sort of less rigid approach would therefore seem to be defensible.

As we've seen, **Plato** justified a "noble lie" (society must be structured a certain way because people are born with different native capacities) for the purposes of promoting the common good (*see* page 25). However, in most other things, Plato would have agreed with Kant: we should not judge the rightness of actions by their consequences. Utilitarianism, of course, does exactly that, and those following in the tradition of Bentham might defend government mendacity by appeal to "the need to protect the populace" (or some such thing). But might this defence not be used to condone *any* degree of lying?

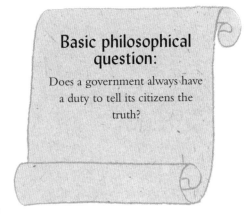

Basic philosophical question:

Does a government always have a duty to tell its citizens the truth?

In *Taking Rights Seriously* (1977), **Ronald Dworkin** considers whether utilitarianism can be reconciled with a concern for fundamental human rights. Using a playing cards metaphor, Dworkin argues that, in situations where utilitarian concerns (e.g. public welfare, the common good) conflict with certain human rights, then "rights are trumps". So, no matter what the beneficial consequences to be had from (say) persecuting some minority group, the

> *"The impersonality suitable for public action...*
> *warrants methods usually excluded for private individuals,*
> *and sometimes it licences ruthlessness."*
> Thomas Nagel

equal right of everyone *not* to be persecuted trumps that benefit. Of course, the question remains as to whether the right not to be lied to is a *fundamental* human right; perhaps (to continue Dworkin's playing card metaphor) it is a "lesser" right that – just as a Jack may be beaten by a Queen – may in turn be beaten by an important utilitarian concern. Could some rights therefore simply be considered as "desirable", not essential? In which case, the government may agree to tell the truth, *as long as* no more fundamental concern (e.g. public safety) trumps that. But wouldn't that undermine the notion of "fundamental rights"? Who would decide the ranking, and how?

Noble lies

We'll return to these questions later (when we look at torture), but it's clear from the above discussion that governments will often find themselves in positions where they are forced to weigh up a simple concern for truth-telling with other important concerns. As the American philosopher **Thomas Nagel** (b. 1937) has argued, the sort of dilemmas that face governments can justify extreme measures and actions that – if you or I were to perform them – may seem immoral or even "ruthless". So, perhaps, not only is your government entitled to lie, but, in the protection of the public, it may go further. All of which may seem like a justification of *any* action – to keep a lid on this "aliens" thing, who knows what lengths the government is prepared to go to? Perhaps you're better off not knowing.

Making a decision:

There must be standards by which a government is to be held accountable by its electorate. But if a government is justified in lying, then why not other actions, too? There is a conflict here: a government exists (supposedly) to protect your rights, but in doing so it can also infringe them! As much as you might like to know the truth about UFOs (or whatever), you will probably have to admit that – even if they were real – the government wouldn't tell you about it.

Should I emigrate to Mars?

Hobbes • Locke • Marx • Nozick • Rawls • Mills

Planet Earth is getting pretty cramped. One day, you see an advert asking for people willing to emigrate to Mars, offering free passage, extensive property and well-paid, secure work to those willing to give up the Terran life. The colony is well established now, and you have a skillset much needed there at the moment. "Why not?" you conclude, and one dreamless hyper-sleep later you arrive.

Mars is greener than you'd expected and your new ranch looks lovely. But all is not as it seems. Unknown to the people back on Earth, the colonists may not be the only inhabitants of the Red Planet. Rumours circulate of elusive, nomadic groups of beings, roaming the Martian wastes. What does that mean? Are you in any danger? Is the land yours, or not?

The right to property

This is a contentious issue. For theorists like **Thomas Hobbes** and **John Locke**, it was a key motive for establishing the social contract. However, the two thinkers differed as to what this meant. Hobbes thought that, in a state of nature, there was no distinction between "mine" and "thine" – property was simply a matter of what each man could get and maintain hold of. Therefore, he argued that property was not a secure right, but one that could be guaranteed only by the sovereign – who could just as easily take it away again. In contrast, Locke thought that, while the state should protect property ownership, it did not have the right to unjustly revoke it – regardless of what the sovereign feels.

Human rights legislation generally agrees with Locke. The *Universal Declaration of Human Rights* (1948) states not only that "Everyone has the right to own property", but furthermore that "No one shall be arbitrarily deprived" of it. Of course, most countries allow for the compulsory purchase of private land (with due compensation) where it is in the public interest (to build a reservoir, perhaps). Under most circumstances, however, governments respect the human right of property ownership.

But what about the native Martians? Don't

I claim this land in the name of Earth!

they have rights? Since they were here first, doesn't the land belong to them? Well, actually, both Hobbes and Locke would probably have sided with the colonists. You may recognize here the obvious parallel with the European colonization of the Americas, among other places. Hobbes thought that the Native Americans "have no government at all, and live at this day in that brutish manner". Thus, Hobbes would probably have considered the indigenous Martians as living in a state of lawlessness, and so – unless they joined in some way with your community – to possess no right to property at all. Similarly, you might use Locke to argue that, because the Martians were a nomadic people, who had grown nothing on the Martian deserts, and had built no permanent structures, the land itself was *terra nullius* (a Latin legal term meaning "no man's land"), and thus fair game. For Locke, it is through the "labor of his body and the work of his hand" that land may pass into a person's possession (*Second Treatise on Civil Government*, 1689). So, plant a few Martian carrots, and it's all yours – for in pursuing a nomadic way of life, the native Martians have failed to stake their claim to it.

Land distribution

But there's something about all of this that seems a bit unjust, don't you think? The indigenous Martians may be nomadic, but wouldn't it be absurd to consider them

Basic philosophical question:

Is there such a thing as a right to property, and on what basis is it held?

effectively to be *trespassers* in their native land? They may have no "civil government" (as defined by Terran democrats), but does that mean that they have no civilization, no laws at all? In such a way, the great European colonial powers used the doctrine of *terra nullius* to justify invasion and land-grab. Whether in Africa, the Americas or Australia, even if they were not nomadic, the country's indigenous people were considered not sufficiently civilized and therefore fit – in their own "best interests", perhaps – to be conquered.

But you're not some thuggish, colonialist land-grabber, are you? If you're to have the right to stay on Mars, you want to do this properly. So, you and some other fair-minded colonists enter into negotiations with the natives, asking for permission to stay. The native Martians are actually pretty peaceful and easy-going, and after learning

"Everyone has the right to own property"
Universal Declaration of Human Rights

a little more of each other's languages and cultures, you begin to discuss some basic rules as to who should be entitled to what. But immediately you hit a problem. While you're in favour of an equal distribution of land, some of your fellow colonists are pretty libertarian and argue that ensuring that everyone has the same amount of land to cultivate would hold back the fledgling Martian economy. They argue that, while things might start off with everyone in possession of equal property, it's natural that some people might want to sell some of their land – some areas may be more fertile than others – while some might want to buy it.

But if you restrict property sales, then isn't this a restriction on personal liberty? And wouldn't you be edging toward some form of state control (some form of communism, or at least some sort of authoritarianism)? But if you allow the property developers free rein, then you sow the seeds of inequality, of divisions between rich and poor, haves and have-nots. Gradually, you come to realize that, while you may have left Earth behind, you've brought with you all of its political dilemmas!

Nozick and Entitlement Theory

We know what **Karl Marx** would do – abolish all private property – but it looks like the free-market capitalists who funded all this aren't on his side. Is there any other way of thinking you could apply in order to establish some sort of fairness?

In arguing against the form of state intervention that you've been considering, the libertarian philosopher **Robert Nozick**

Nozick's Entitlement Theory of Justified Ownership

1. The principle of acquisition

Only certain types of property can be owned, and these should be acquired according to just principles.

2. The principle of transfer

Property must be bought, exchanged or given in the right way.

3. The principle of rectification

If property has not been acquired or transferred properly, there should be compensation for the victims.

argues that, even where there isn't complete equality of wealth and property, we may still have a society where people may be said to be entitled to their possessions. His Entitlement Theory argues that it's fine for people to have different amounts of property, to be free to buy and sell, as long as all this activity abides by certain rules. Nozick therefore takes a *historical* view of property rights: ownership is justified *if* (a) the property was acquired properly; (b) it was (if applicable) transferred in the right way; and (c) if there have been any contraventions

"Labour being the unquestionable Property of the Labourer, no man but he can have a right to what that is once joyned to"

Locke

of (a) or (b), due rectifications have been observed. This appears fair (if not egalitarian), for it seems to rule out the sort of unfair land-grabbing that you want to guard against. If it means that some profit more from speculating, then – well, that's just commerce!

Now, let's look at your Martian ranch. Does your possession of it meet Nozick's criteria? The problem is that Nozick's theory seems to ignore the question of *terra nullius* for indigenous peoples – or, rather, the hypothetical "state of nature" from which we are asked to apply his Entitlement Theory seems to assume an equal basis for all parties. But this is not the case, for the Martians may *already* be said to be in "possession" of their land – or, at least, to have a greater claim to it than you do. But Nozick's theory is not alone in this blindness, for, although he argues to a different, "fairer" outcome, so

does **John Rawls** (*see* page 46). Both, in fact, take as their starting point a hypothetical group of people whose property rights are guaranteed by virtue of being parties to a social contract. But, regarding the Martians, any such agreement would seem to gloss over the awkward question of how they went from inhabitants of their native land to citizens with limited property rights. But why should they share it at all? Weren't they there first? Why should they accept the liberal democratic ideals that Locke, Nozick or Rawls would seek to impose on them? As the Jamaican philosopher **Charles W Mills** (b. 1951) points out, it's not so much that Nozick and Rawls deliberately reject this problem, but rather that they simply fail to account for it: "In effect, Rawls and Nozick assume *terra nullius*, ignoring the genocide and expropriation of native peoples."

Making a decision:

However you justify it, and whatever distribution of property you ultimately determine as "fair", your very presence on Mars would seem to be problematic. It's likely that the Martians will have evolved very different notions to you – regarding property and ownership, how laws are established, the notion of rights – in fact, it's possible that they have radically different conceptions of individuality. While I'm not suggesting that the difference between indigenous populations and early European "settlers" was as radical, it's still obvious that any attempt by the settlers to justify their presence in their own terms (e.g. social contract theories or *terra nullius*) would be culturally biased. Wouldn't it be better – fairer – to seek permission for settlement and property on the terms of the native inhabitants?

Can I sack a robot?

Kant • Bostrom • Yudkowsy • Searle • Dennett

You come home from a hard day's work, and nothing has been done – the laundry isn't ironed, the dishes are unwashed, and, from the forlorn look on its face, you doubt very much that the dog has been walked. You go into the servant's quarters. "What's going on?" you ask. "Historical records indicate a temporary cessation of productive activity to be the most fitting response to unsatisfactory conditions," comes the response. "What?!" "The vernacular equivalent would be 'going on strike'." "But ...you're a robot!"

Such a scenario may resemble a slightly corny futuristic sit-com or some 1950s pulp sci-fi, but the point it raises is an important one: on what basis does a being possess rights? In fact, some futurists already claim that, regarding artificial intelligence (AI), the issue will soon cease to be academic. In January 2017 the European Union even went as far as issuing a draft report suggesting a set of regulations regarding "electronic personhood" for sufficiently advanced AIs. At this moment, this is more of a "legal fiction" (in the same way that we treat companies as "persons"). However, as machines become more complicated and unpredictable, might we one day – as envisaged in Isaac Asimov's *Bicentennial Man* (1976) – grant a robot personhood?

What makes a "person"?

If we adopt the sort of approach already outlined by **Immanuel Kant**, then we may argue that, in order to possess rights, an individual must, at the very least, be a *person*. But how should we define personhood? This is a complicated philosophical issue, and subject to some controversy, but most philosophers would say that there are a set of features that must be possessed: a person thinks and feels, is able (in some way) to use language to communicate and express themselves, has beliefs and motives, is a social being with ties to family and friends. Each of us may possess these qualities in different ways or to varying extents, and we may quibble about the exact list, but most would agree that something like the above is what is generally meant when we talk of "persons".

"It is wrong to inflict pain on a mouse, unless there are sufficiently strong morally overriding reasons to do so. The same would hold for any sentient AI system."
Nick Bostrom and Eliezer Yudkowsky

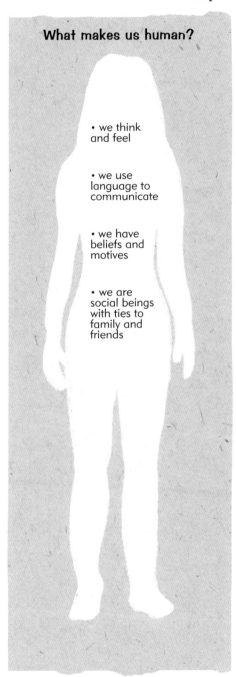

What makes us human?

- we think and feel

- we use language to communicate

- we have beliefs and motives

- we are social beings with ties to family and friends

For Kant, of course, it is the fact that, above all, we are *rational* beings with *autonomy* (self-control and independence), for it is the frustration of rational goals that rights are meant to guard against (*see* page 24).

So, by these criteria, is your striking robot a "person"? Well, as things stand, only the most hopeful futurist would claim personhood for any currently existing robot or AI. There are, arguably, no machines that "think" or "feel" in the commonly accepted fullest sense of these terms, and none that has the degree of autonomy that we might accord even to young children. That said, a number of philosophers argue that it is a mere matter of time, and soon – depending on whom you ask – we shall be forced to answer some awkward moral questions about our relationships with machines (in more senses than one, if we consider the current developments in "sexbots"!).

But surely, you say, isn't a machine just a machine? If it doesn't work, or decides to "go on strike", what's to stop you taking a baseball bat to it? Well, what *would* stop you? Presumably, you wouldn't do the same to an animal. This point is jointly made by the Swedish philosopher **Nick Bostrom** (b. 1973) and American AI researcher **Eliezer Yudkowsky** (b. 1979) ("The Ethics of Artificial Intelligence", 2011), who argue that a "sentient AI system, even if it lacks language and other higher cognitive faculties, is not like a stuffed toy animal or a windup doll; it is more like a living animal." Therefore, if it is wrong to cause pain to a living animal, the same should apply to "any sentient AI system." But that begs the question: could a sufficiently complex machine actually feel pain? It may be so complicated that it might be difficult to know – and how do you *really* know that other human beings feel pain in the way you do? We observe others' behaviour. If a machine were to behave as if it were in pain, then who's to say it isn't? The fact that it's made of metal and plastic is neither here nor there – as Bostrom and Yudkowsy argue, "it makes no moral difference whether a being is made of silicon or carbon, or whether its brain uses semi conductors or neurotransmitters."

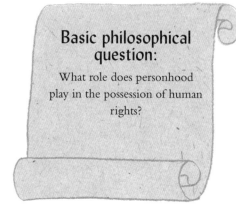

Basic philosophical question:

What role does personhood play in the possession of human rights?

Are we all zombies?

Key to this issue is something called *qualia*, or the various qualities we subjectively experience as we think and feel. Such qualities are difficult to communicate and may even be "beyond words" – how could you describe the smell of coffee to someone who'd never experienced it, or the colour red? Sceptics such as the American philosopher **John Searle** (b. 1932) therefore argue that machines can never be conscious in this way, because such properties – as far as we know – are experienced only by living, organic beings. The fact that a machine could be programmed to *behave* as if it had these experiences is neither here nor there, for, unless their artificial brains in some way could *recreate* human consciousness, then all such behaviour would merely be for show. For Searle, although machines may *appear* to understand language (or chess, or Go, or quiz shows), in reality, they do not. If Searle

is right, then – unless neuroscientists really crack the mystery of consciousness, and can recreate it – robots and machines will never be persons, in the fullest sense, for they will lack sentience.

Are we zombies?

human being   zombie

Judged by external behaviour, both have thoughts, feelings, emotions, decisions and actions. If zombies (or robots) only lack qualia, then need we presume they exist?

> *"My car and my adding machine...understand nothing: they are not in that line of business."*
> John Searle

However, not everyone agrees, and some – such as American philosopher **Daniel Dennett** (b. 1942) – even argue that qualia do not exist. What we think of as conscious experience, Dennett argues, is actually just an illusion, one of many comforting lies that our brain tells itself in order to further our evolutionary development. Do you think that you are the same person as yesterday, or that all the different (and often contrary) thoughts and feelings you have are part of the same coherent self? Dennett takes aim at the treasured notion of the mental self as a separate, consistent, unified ego, and argues

that not only is this view false, but so is the idea that we have conscious experiences (qualia). We are, merely, purely physical, complex, biological machines.

But wouldn't this make us unconscious "zombies"? "Are zombies possible? They're not just possible, they're actual. We're all zombies. Nobody is conscious" (*Consciousness Explained*, 1991). So, if human beings are no more than "zombies" (non-sentient machines mistakenly believing they have qualia), then so are the robots, and no less deserving of "human" rights than you or I.

Making a decision:

Whether you can sack your industrial-action-taking robot depends on whether it can be considered a person, for only persons are employed or sacked (or wrongfully dismissed); machines are bought, rented, returned or junked. The question of artificial personhood, which seems far-fetched at the moment, may soon be a real issue. When it is, the question of "qualia" and related notions will take centre stage. We know that machines can best us in what were once considered strictly human endeavours (calculating, analysing, organizing), but many philosophers still think that the inability of machines to feel pain will rule them out from full qualification for "human-like" rights – assuming, of course, that qualia do exist, and that it's not all just in your head.

Should my right to vote be based on my IQ?

Caplan • Mill • Kant • Singer • Descartes

It's election time again. However, rather than use their democratic right to bring about meaningful change, the populace elects a candidate who ran a campaign based on fear, manipulation and – let's be frank – lies. Running as a "man of the people" fighting the "fat cats" of finance and the "liberal elite", a moment's Googling reveals that he is nothing of the sort – a product of a similarly privileged elite and a mere front for rich business interests. Can't they see that they've been played? Sometimes, you wonder if some people deserve the right to vote at all.

So what do you suggest? Some voting equivalent of a driving test? That it should be based on IQ, or level of education? In *The Myth of the Rational Voter* (2007), the American economist **Bryan Caplan** (b. 1971) argues for just such a change, citing evidence that many people vote based on irrational prejudices, biases and misunderstandings. If voters had to pass a test on basic economic issues, wouldn't this result in more sensible policies and reduce the power of unscrupulous politicians to manipulate our fears?

Rights and rationality

The problem is that such moves are equivalent to limiting the right to have an opinion – and isn't everyone entitled to that? Furthermore, having struggled so hard to achieve universal suffrage, we should think very carefully before once again limiting it. But Caplan is not alone in this view, and – as we've seen – while favouring the broadening of the right to vote for women, **John Stuart**

Mill was nonetheless sceptical about the ability of the general public to make best use of that right. Shouldn't the better educated get more votes? But that risks promoting the very form of elitism that democracy is designed to counteract, and raises awkward questions about ensuring that everyone has equal access to that education, and that such tests are fair and free of bias.

If, as **Immanuel Kant** argues, we must allot rights based on an individual's possession of a certain rational capacity (*see* page 123), then what about those who do not meet that standard? We already limit the voting right according to age for the reason that those below 18 (16 or 21, in some countries) are not considered sufficiently mature to consider such important questions. But, as public surveys regularly reveal, an alarming percentage of citizens in the major democracies are unable to answer quite basic political questions. If a bright ten-year-old can name the three traditional divisions of democratic government, and a forty-year-old

136

cannot, should we grant the right to vote to the former and withdraw it from the latter? But, bright as the ten-year-old might be, she may also lack the life experience – first-hand knowledge of the world of work, of lived history and of other valuable things that contribute to a fuller picture of the world – possessed by the forty-year-old. Perhaps, then, an overemphasis on intellectual knowledge would be a bad thing for democracy.

Humans and animals

But Kant's notion of who deserves rights is problematic in other ways. As the Australian philosopher **Peter Singer** (b. 1946) has argued, if we are to base rights on mental capacity, then "the life of a newborn is of less value than the life of a pig, a dog, or a chimpanzee", for human babies "are not born self-aware, or capable of grasping that they exist over time. They are not persons." If, as sometimes unfortunately happens, such infants never develop full personhood, perhaps less so than certain primates, or dolphins, or other animals, then why should we grant rights to such humans and not to those animals? I'm not, of course, suggesting that chimpanzees should get the vote, but this sliding scale of personhood raises the question of how rights are allotted, and whether all humans should possess them equally.

> **Basic philosophical question:**
> Should the right to vote be universal, or subject to certain criteria?

Kant gets around this problem by arguing that – for instance – while animals cannot possess rights, we nonetheless have a moral duty to treat them decently because it reflects on our *own* moral character – ill treatment would breed bad moral qualities. Presumably, this would also apply to humans with some form of cognitive impairment, which would seem to imply that we possess only an *indirect* duty to certain humans. You can see how Kant's account sets a high standard for rights that is potentially worrying: an indirect duty to animals would not seem to necessitate vegetarianism, so one may wonder what such a duty would look like when applied to certain classes of human.

A different approach to rights could take a religious approach. The French philosopher **René Descartes** (1596–1650) famously

> *"I think, therefore I am."*
> René Descartes

considered the defining quality of a person to be the capacity for self-reflective thought – "I think, therefore I am" – and many other Renaissance and Enlightenment philosophers held similar opinions. For Descartes, it was the possession of a "rational soul" that distinguished us from animals – which were, he argued, mere "machines", lacking any real sentience or self-awareness. Most evolutionary biologists would now disagree with this view, arguing that we are much closer to animals than Descartes supposed. All of which seems to leave the waters muddier than before.

Making a decision:

If we base the right to vote on education or the possession of a certain basic knowledge, then a great many people will be deprived of it (while others not currently granted it may gain it). More fundamentally, basing rights on possession of rational capacity may lead to distasteful consequences. Perhaps, then, human rights should be granted universally on some other basis, and we should rather look to other means of improving democracy – such as better educating the electorate and curbing media disinformation and manipulation.

There is a bomb somewhere. To what lengths should I go to find it?

Kant • Bentham • Hampshire • Machiavelli • Ginbar

It's a familiar dilemma, beloved of Hollywood screenwriters and thriller novelists: a terrorist has planted a bomb somewhere; if you don't find it, innocents will die; you've caught one of those responsible, but he refuses to talk. What will you do?

If you respect the man's human rights not to be subjected to "torture or to cruel, inhuman or degrading treatment or punishment" (as the *Universal Declaration of Human Rights* puts it), then you risk the lives of many more. The utilitarian argument is therefore clear: the needs of the many outweigh those of the few. But, as we've seen, utilitarianism is a dubious basis for human rights, seeming sometimes to justify actions that appear morally repugnant. But what is moral about letting innocents die to protect the rights of the guilty few? Let's say, then, that you torture him, and that you get him to talk. Can you rely on the information? Even the innocent have been found to "confess" under torture, just to make it stop, and of course he might lie. And in doing so you lose the moral high ground: you can no longer distinguish yourself from the terrorist in terms of your respect for human life.

Duties and consequences

In legal and political philosophy, this is known as a *ticking bomb scenario* (TBS). In this debate, we may take **Immanuel Kant** as representing one extreme – the absolute protection of human rights – and **Jeremy Bentham** the other – that rights may on occasion be overridden by a consideration for consequences. Kant's position is an example of what's called *deontology*, which sees morality in terms of *duty*. For Kant, we

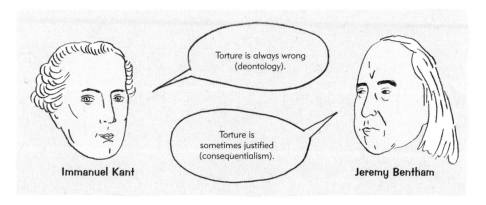

Torture is always wrong (deontology).

Torture is sometimes justified (consequentialism).

Immanuel Kant

Jeremy Bentham

Is torture ever justified?

✓ Pros	✗ Cons
more likely to get information	subject may lie or say anything
may save lives	question of certainty (the subject may be innocent)
suspension of human rights is justified by outcome	loss of respect for human life

follow moral rules not out of self-interest (or some other proposed consequence of our actions), but for their own sake – that is what being moral amounts to (*see* page 125). In contrast, Bentham's position is an example of *consequentialism*, which sees morality in terms of the outcomes of actions; things are not in themselves "good" or "bad", but may be considered so in light of the consequences. Not all consequentialists share Bentham's utilitarianism – some might argue for the action producing the greatest amount of *fairness* or *justice*, for example – and not all deontologists share Kant's absolutism about moral duties. However, the two philosophers may be made to stand for the two poles of our debate.

In this TBS, it's obvious that the absolute protection of human rights could result in the mass death of innocents. However, while it may seem straight forward to inflict pain on a guilty man intent on evil, it is less obvious that a *suspected* terrorist should be tortured. A consequentialist approach might still justify such an action, but it would seem less morally clear: what if he were innocent, or a case of mistaken identity? Some of the alleged terrorists kept by the American government in the naval base in Guantánamo Bay in Cuba have been released without charge, having arguably suffered such infringements upon their human rights. If it was ultimately decided that those individuals were innocent, then doesn't that question the decision of the state to suspend those rights in the first place? Doesn't that uncertainty as to guilt weaken the consequentialist position?

There is also the issue of what such actions might lead to. If a TBS can justify arrest without charge, torture or other rights contraventions, then doesn't this represent a slippery slope? Might it not lead to an

Basic philosophical question:

Should the right not to suffer torture always be respected?

> *"[N]o one shall be subjected to torture or to cruel, inhuman or degrading treatment or punishment."*
> Universal Declaration of Human Rights

over-powerful "terror" state, armed with the capacity to routinely detain, interrogate and torture its citizens on whatever grounds it saw fit? To grant the state such powers would seem to divorce it from common standards of morality. As with truthfulness (considered earlier), it would seem to lead to a situation where it is fine for the state to act in such a way that would be immoral, even criminal, if those actions were performed by any individual citizen.

The lesser of two evils

But perhaps we are wrong here in seeking to apply standards of personal morality ("It's wrong to torture") to the public sphere. Should governments be bound at all by moral concerns? To do so would seem to restrict their ability to make decisions in the interests of its citizens, especially when dealing with other states who do not scruple to bend and break moral rules. As the British philosopher **Stuart Hampshire** (1914–

2004) argued, "it seems unavoidable that, in the exercise of political power, one should very often, perhaps usually, be choosing between two evils, and trying to prevent the greater misery and the worse injustice". **Niccolò Machiavelli** would agree. In fact, he considered being bound by personal morality – as desirable as that would be – to be a liability for a ruler, creating a weakness that others could exploit.

But perhaps in all of this the fundamental worry is what terrorism is making us become. In *Why Not Torture Terrorists?* (2008), **Yuval Ginbar**, legal adviser to Amnesty International, surveys much of the above debate before concluding that there is more at stake here than the protection of life, or worries regarding certainty; fundamentally, resorting to torture risks making us less human. So, while "we should do everything in our power" to save lives, we should also ensure that this "does not involve losing our own humanity".

Making a decision:

While some argue that there would seem to be justifiable reasons to suspend human rights under certain hypothetical circumstances, in practice the issue is frequently not so clear cut. Aside from questions of certainty and the moral slippery slope that it leads to, torture would seem to represent more than a loss of human rights, but a loss of what it means to be human.

I am a teacher who's a part-time nude model – is that a problem?

Locke • Mill • Warren • Brandeis • Prosser • Thomson • Bork

You work as a teacher. One day, you are called into the headteacher's office, and she informs you that some "matters" have come to her attention regarding your conduct outside of work. Specifically, she has found out that you have been doing some nude modelling on the side. Since you're good at your job, she's "willing to overlook the matter", as long as you give it up. She is also going to discipline you for "bringing the school into disrepute". Is this fair?

In case you question the likelihood of this scenario, in 2016 there were two separate cases of teachers (one male, one female) moonlighting as lingerie models – I'll leave you to work out which one was sacked…

The Universal Declaration of Human Rights protects both privacy and the right not to be discriminated against for legal sexual orientation and conduct, and free expression. Liberals such as John Locke and John Stuart Mill attempted to draw a strict line between the private and public spheres, protecting the individual from the intrusion of state and society. A bit of nude life modelling is therefore well within your rights.

The right to a private life

In 1890 the American lawyers **Samuel Warren** (1852–1910) and **Louis Brandeis** (1856–1941) attempted to define a more formal "right to be let alone" in matters of no public concern, where it can be seen as an extension of the right to property: just as you own your body and person, you should also possess rights regarding your likeness and information about yourself.

The US legal scholar **William Prosser** (1898–1972) argued similarly ("Privacy", 1960), identifying four ways in which privacy should be protected: (1) intrusion into solitude or private affairs, (2) revelation of embarrassing private facts, (3) false, damaging publicity, and (4) use of one's likeness for another's purpose (e.g. using a photo of you in an advert without your consent). You can see here that (1) and (2) are the most relevant to your situation. Could you therefore argue that the headteacher's actions represent an invasion of your right to privacy?

Of course, you may not feel embarrassed by your modelling activities – if you're comfortable enough taking off your clothes for strangers, then probably not. It may cause some titters and whispers in the classroom, but they need to get over it – after all, their own art room brims with nudes by Michelangelo and Matisse. The human body is nothing to be ashamed of. Perhaps then the issue is not your extracurricular activities, but the prudishness and hypocrisy of the school and its governors.

Let's say that a company hires a well-known footballer to publicize its brand, but that the (married) footballer is shortly after discovered to be having an affair. Extramarital relations are not in themselves illegal, of course, but perhaps the company wishes to promote a "family-friendly" image, so decides to release the footballer from his contract. In this case, perhaps there is a clause in the contract that allows the company to sack the footballer for any reason they like (thereby forestalling any actions for discrimination or wrongful termination). But teachers' contracts may not be so accommodating, so a justifiable reason for termination may have to be given.

The question, then, is whether your actions can in some way be considered sufficiently "disreputable" to bring the school into "disrepute". However, as a legal question, this may be decided differently in different countries and at different times. Questions of moral conduct, where no illegal action has occurred, therefore represent a shifting standard, and – as with questions of censorship – involve judgments of "taste" (your teaching contract may contain some suitably vague clause stipulating your adherence to a "code of conduct"). Whether an organization has a right to discipline or terminate an employee according to its own interpretation of that standard is therefore a tricky question, and one that often ends up in court.

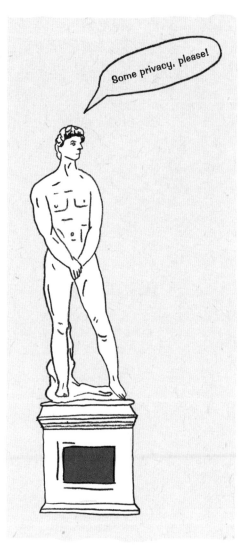

"All human beings have three lives: public, private, and secret."
Gabriel García Márquez

Problems with privacy

So is privacy your strongest defence? It's not as if you publicized the fact, or posted images on social media. The modelling sessions take place privately, and are organized and attended only by adults. How then is it anyone else's business? While you might appeal to a "right to privacy", others have argued that no such right actually exists. The American philosopher **Judith Jarvis Thomson** (b. 1929) has argued that what we think of as privacy is actually a *collection* of other rights – to property, security and so forth. Similarly, the American judge **Robert Bork** (1927–2012) argued that there is no direct constitutional basis for privacy, which is better protected in terms of liberty. In other words, you are better off arguing that your life modelling is a form of free personal expression.

The issue is not that life modelling is illegal – you're legally free to pursue it – but one concerning the more nebulous sphere of "respectability". As a teacher, you are a role model for your pupils, and so your actions – private or public – should embody higher moral standards; which, perhaps, is fair enough – but *whose* standards?

> ## Basic philosophical question:
> Is there such a thing as a right to privacy?

Another problem with the notion of a right to privacy is that it would seem to come into direct conflict with the "public right to know" or "freedom of information". Again, there is much debate about whether this in itself is an absolute "right", and if so whether it is relative (as we saw in the discussion concerning government truthfulness). This criticism often arises in response to accusations of press intrusion. If privacy were defended in a more robust way, then it would damage democracy – how would we learn of dishonest politicians, business corruption or other issues considered "in

"Men born to freedom are naturally alert to repel invasion of their liberty by evil-minded rulers. The greatest dangers to liberty lurk in insidious encroachment by men of zeal, well-meaning but without understanding."
Louis D Brandeis

the public interest"? If the press were solely concerned with such good causes, then this argument might carry more weight, but often it is wheeled out as a defence of their search for the sort of titillating gossip and personal scandal that sells newspapers. It is true, however, that any privacy legislation that restricted powers of investigation and publication would also restrict reporting of more serious concerns.

A shrinking sphere

So privacy, like freedom, is a double-edged sword. And yet it's also true that the private sphere is shrinking – it's not uncommon now for prospective employers or university admissions tutors to browse the social media profiles of applicants, and employees are frequently sacked for expressing views or publicizing activities that they considered "private". How did

your headteacher find out? Someone blabbed or "shared", no doubt. "Privacy" is therefore increasingly synonymous with "secrecy" – and our hi-tech world is gradually ensuring that there is less and less of that.

Making a decision:

Your dilemma reveals an area of conflict between the public and private spheres. As Mill argued, morality should be defined only in terms of our duty to others, not by some vague standard of "goodness" or "respectability", and furthermore should fundamentally protect individual freedom. The problem is that privacy is shrinking, while the distinctions between public and private – and what you are "allowed" to do in either – are insufficiently clear.

My beliefs are in conflict with my job. What should I do?

Rawls • Locke • Mill • Popper • Kuhn

You're back in front of the headteacher – what have you done this time? It concerns the school curriculum. She'd like to remind you that, as a private institution, the school has a tradition of fostering religious belief, and she just wants to ensure that you're doing your part. Has she mistaken you for the Religious Studies teacher? What has this got to do with biology? "Well, it's come to my attention", she says, "that you are not teaching *alternative* theories to evolution." *Creationism?* Is that even a *theory?* And why should you have a duty to teach it? Isn't that a matter of faith?

We've seen **John Rawls** argue that individual freedom is best served if the state stays neutral regarding questions of "the good" – that is, concerning subjective values and personal life choices. Similarly, **John Locke**'s *Letter Concerning Toleration* (1689) argues that government should stay out of private matters, concerning itself only with "civil interests" – the protection of health, security and "the possession of outward things, such as money, lands, houses. However, as already noted, while Rawls and Locke might like to treat religious belief as a private matter, it has obvious public aspects that may conflict with "neutral" state policy: permitting people a choice to do a particular thing (e.g. abortion) may go against the views of those who are against it happening *at all* (i.e. pro-lifers). But, on the whole, such *pluralism* at least allows each to make his or her own decision.

Learning about all sides

However, concerning matters of education, the dilemma is slightly different, because teachers do not always enable choice *between* competing systems or world views, but rather teach from *within* one. **John Stuart Mill** argued that the goals of education would in fact be better served if a wider range of competing views *were* taught, because it would foster greater individual powers of critical analysis. Some curricula no doubt provide this to an extent, but there are still many areas where – even if the teacher were inclined – there is no time to consider alternative views. And, besides, isn't that what university-level study is for? Of course, the counterargument runs, by that time the damage is already done: most of our fundamental beliefs are formed in childhood, and though we may question them, our views tend to fall into line with those of family and peers. Education is therefore an important formative process and school age a vital period where all sides are heard.

We considered the virtues (and flaws) of secular multiculturalism earlier, but the more specific issue here is whether the

Good tests kill flawed theories; we remain alive to guess again.

Normal science does not aim at novelties of fact or theory and, when successful, finds none.

Karl Popper

Thomas Kuhn

right to tolerance of one's views and to freedom of belief necessitates that *all* beliefs should be given equal weighting, especially in educational settings. Does creationism have a *right* to be taught *as a theory*? Scientists (and certain believers) who argue that it doesn't have that right point to the differing nature of scientific and religious truth: science works from observation to hypothesis to experiment to conclusion, working with facts and data; religion deals with revelation, with spiritual truths and moral questions. But this is really Locke's "private sphere" argument restated: religious belief is a personal matter that need not conflict with public discourse. And yet, while they are generally more subtle than the caricature of a world created 6,000 years ago in 7 days, many creationist views are still arguably at odds with the scientific mainstream, believers in which see them as providing alternative scientific accounts. How then can such views be merely personal and private?

"The commonwealth seems to me to be a society of men constituted only for the procuring, preserving, and advancing of their own civil interests."
John Locke

> "The scientific enterprise as a whole does from time to time prove useful, open up new territory, display order, and test long-accepted belief. Nevertheless, the individual engaged on a normal research problem is almost never doing any one of these things."
> Thomas Kuhn

Are religion and science so different?

On the other side, some philosophers have questioned the view that science is the dispassionate, rational search for factual truth. **Karl Popper** painted a picture of science as moving methodically through a process of advancing and testing hypotheses, refining or rejecting false theories in the light of evidence. But this model was questioned by the American philosopher **Thomas Kuhn** (1822–96), who suggested rather that scientific theories often advance by less rational means – by guesswork, or leaps of intuition, by ignoring counter-evidence for the sake of making progress within a unified

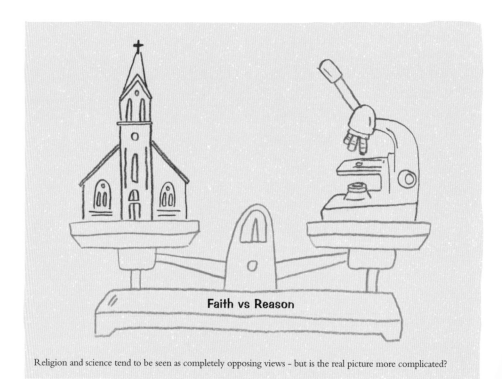

Faith vs Reason

Religion and science tend to be seen as completely opposing views - but is the real picture more complicated?

discipline. The theory that the Sun revolves around the Earth wasn't abandoned because it was suddenly seen to be wrong, but also because of a combination of other factors – social, religious, political. False theories aren't abandoned at one go, and rather than the bold search for new hypotheses, scientific theories more resemble joint beliefs holding the community of scientists together, allowing "puzzle solving" within a framework of unquestioned assumptions.

Fundamental change happens only at rare turning points, when anomalies become too numerous – and revolution occurs. Of course, science isn't merely another form of belief, but, if Kuhn is right, and religious views also contain public, factual assertions, then the traditional opposition

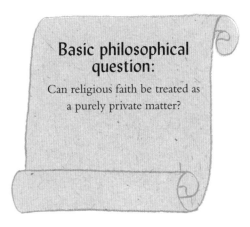

Basic philosophical question:

Can religious faith be treated as a purely private matter?

between religion and science, between rational and irrational, public and private, breaks down.

Making a decision:

You could put yourself on either side of this debate – perhaps the school want to make you teach something that goes against your faith. As I imply, independent schools may have greater powers to evolve a curriculum that differs in content and emphasis from that prescribed for state schools. However, for any educational qualifications to have general currency, they will need to meet certain standards – a certificate in "Christian Biology" is unlikely to carry any weight. Perhaps then you might suggest that, while these topics deserve equal hearing, a course in science (intended to qualify you for entrance to other institutions) is not the best place. What about in philosophy class? You do run that, right?

Justice

Chapter 5

Should I drink fair-trade coffee?

McLuhan • Klein • Smith • Marx

You are a citizen of the world – in more ways than one. You work on an American-designed laptop manufactured in China. You're drinking "Italian" coffee that's actually made from beans imported from Africa and South America, ground locally. Your T-shirt is from Honduras and your jeans are from Cambodia. Your most recent meal contained peppers grown in Spain and green beans from – Egypt? Really? Even the books you read on the train to work – regardless of the author's or publisher's origins – are prepared and printed in places such as China, the Philippines or India. But is all this a *good* thing? Should you care where the things you buy come from?

We live in an age of *globalization* – or, as Canadian media analyst **Marshall McLuhan** (1911–80) put it, "a global village". With remarkable prescience, McLuhan predicted the drastic "shrinking" effect that electronic media and communication would have upon our lives. Long before the internet, he identified that our sense of who we are and what we care about was being changed by our increasing ability to instantaneously engage with people and events whole continents away. This has had numerous beneficial effects: politically and environmentally, we are now far more aware of scandals and injustices, and electronic media allow us to communicate, organize and mobilize with people we have never met but who share our concerns and goals. Even in terms of produce and trade, it may be argued that the fact that in most supermarkets you can now choose between sushi, fajitas, tortellini or chow mein is a *good* thing; such options make us more aware of other cultures, broaden our tastes, and foster interaction and mutual understanding. But before you congratulate yourself that every different plate of food you eat is a blow against xenophobia and racial intolerance, you should also be aware that globalization has its downside.

Brand invasion

In *No Logo* (2000), the Canadian writer and activist **Naomi Klein** (b. 1970) laid bare the negative effects of globalization hidden behind the shiny exterior. In it, she charts the growth of "the brand", its growing ubiquity, invading private and public spaces alike, pasting over individual cultures and traditions with shallow, glossy uniformity. And yet, we feel powerless to respond – what can we do? If, as she argues, we are unable to stand up to corporations, then democracy and free speech are put in doubt.

But it's not just the pervasiveness of corporations that is the problem. While

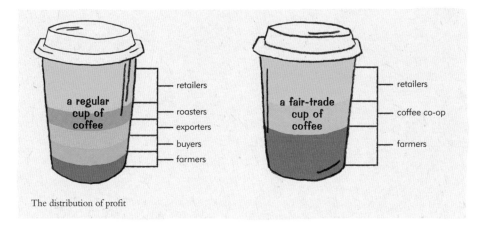

The distribution of profit

brands attempt to create associations of exclusivity and quality, the production of their commodities often takes place in developing-world "sweatshops", where labour is cheap and plentiful, health and safety laws less exacting, and union representation practically non-existent. Recent scandals involving some technology manufacturers reveal that such issues have not gone away, as low wages and exploitative working conditions are alleged to have contributed to a number of worker suicides. Similar problems relate to the mining of tin, an essential ingredient in smartphone and tablet manufacture, where, in such places as Indonesia, there is not just a concern for working conditions and safety, but also the impact on the environment – deforestation, soil erosion, the pollution of rivers and seas. But what can you, the consumer, do?

Applying pressure

One answer is *fair trade*. In working to guarantee that producers are paid a fair wage, fair-trade organizations attempt to eliminate the one-way, exploitative relationship that commonly exists between large multinational companies and their suppliers in developing countries, while ensuring that producers meet acceptable standards relating to working conditions and environmental guidelines. In buying produce marked "fair trade", even if it costs a little bit more, you are therefore using your consumer power to help improve corporate policies and practices. But is this enough? There are, admittedly, some drawbacks to the fair-trade system. For instance, if you're a very poor farmer, then you may not have the means to meet the basic requirements for fair-trade certification – what if eco-friendly pesticides are too

"The human family now exists under conditions of a global village."
Marshall McLuhan

expensive? Also, there are concerns that the extra money from fair trade doesn't always filter down to the workers at the bottom, or out into the community for social projects (as it was intended to).

We might therefore argue that consumer power is not enough. After all, it's easy for a large clothing firm to put out an "ethical clothing line" while continuing to utilize non-ethical manufacturing for its main output. Isn't the answer then to put pressure on companies through increased regulation? This has happened to an extent, especially in environmental terms, but there still seems to be a cross-spectrum reluctance by Western governments to increase business regulation. As pointed out earlier, though such governments may invoke **Adam Smith** and the necessity of free trade, Smith himself

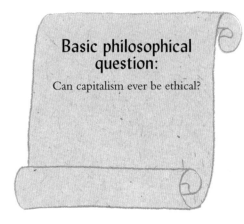

Basic philosophical question:

Can capitalism ever be ethical?

Coffee made from beans grown in South America

Clothes made in Cambodia and Honduras

Laptop designed in the US and made in China

would never have supported international outsourcing or the lack of regulation that currently exists (*see* pages 35–6). But the real reason is fear: if governments press too hard to get multinational corporations to pay taxes, or to meet certain ethical standards concerning foreign manufacture, then there's the danger that such companies may outsource even more of their business, leaving the country in question poorer in both taxes and jobs. This is an understandable (though not exactly commendable) position, but as worry over working conditions and environmental matters become global concerns, and average living standards continue to rise, won't there come a point where such unethical companies will eventually have nowhere left to exploit?

A contradiction in terms?

This dream of market pressures forcing capitalism to become ethical may seem utopian, and arguably does not address the root of the problem. The fundamental issue,

> *"When we lack the ability to talk back to entities that are culturally and politically powerful, the very foundations of free speech and democratic society are called into question."*
> Naomi Klein

as **Karl Marx** argued, is not "fairness", but "alienation" (*see* page 40). The great irony is that the very forces of globalization that have made a vast range of luxury products available and affordable to the population of wealthy countries, enabling them to connect globally, have also ensured that the average sweatshop worker is so poorly paid that he cannot even afford to purchase the product he is making. For Marx, "ethical capitalism" is a contradiction in terms: capitalism can never be ethical, because exploitation and alienation are built into the system – they are what make it work.

Making a decision:

Fair trade might not be a perfect solution, but you should definitely support it (or something like it), for it has produced many genuine benefits, not the least of these being the greater awareness of the issues that now exists. The same is true of consumer power: companies are very sensitive to bad publicity, and while boycotts, petitions and social media campaigns may have only a small impact on the company purse, all have been shown to have some effect in shaping policy. Ultimately, companies want to create a positive brand; you might feel insignificant in relation to your average multinational, but you can make its concern for its brand work in your favour. If we can pressure corporations in such ways, then we can also do the same for governments – which we may also influence through the ballot box. Whether such efforts will ever make capitalism completely ethical is uncertain, but no more so than Marx's dream of complete worker equality – and at least ethical capitalism doesn't require a complete global revolution.

Should I support my country going to war?

Cicero • Augustine • Aquinas • Hobbes

Relations between your country and its neighbour have been worsening for quite a while now. Tensions over border disputes, fuelled by differences in religion and culture, and a long and troubled shared history, have brought matters to boiling point. On a diplomatic mission to your neighbour to promote peace, one of your government's ambassadors is assassinated by a gunman claiming links with your neighbour's ultra-nationalist party. In retaliation, some of your own citizens have resorted to violent protest, attacking your neighbour's embassy. Suddenly, the jingoistic press of both nations are baying for blood. Is war inevitable? Justified? As a citizen, what policy should you support?

The search to establish criteria for *just war* goes back – in Europe, at least – to ancient Greece and Rome, and generally focuses on two aspects: justifications *for* war, and prescriptions for conduct *in* war. In *On Duty*, the Roman philosopher, statesman and orator **Marcus Tullius Cicero** (106–43 BCE) argued that war was only permissible when discussions had failed, and after an official demand for recompense for wrongdoing had not been met. If force *were* to be used, then it should be only of sufficient extent to make the aggressor regret their actions, and to deter any future recurrence – no more. Even where the war is fiercely fought, unarmed civilians should not be engaged and the rights of prisoners of war should be respected.

Regarding your country's dilemma, therefore, Cicero would advise that you first talk to your neighbour. Your government did not authorize your citizens to attack the foreign embassy, and it may be that the

actions of the assassin were something not condoned by your neighbour's leaders either. For, "the man who is not legally a soldier has no right to be fighting the foe", and independent agents (even if they are citizens or patriots) do not represent the state.

Fighting for peace

Cicero's ideas were later developed by the Christian theologian **Saint Augustine** (354–430 CE), who similarly argued that "We do not seek peace in order to be at war, but we go to war that we may have peace" (*Letter* 189). Unlike Cicero, whose philosophical training equipped him with a healthy but open-minded scepticism regarding the pagan religions of his day, war presented for Augustine a special type of problem. On the one hand, he was pragmatic enough to admit that war was sometimes inevitable – even if only for self-defence; on the other hand, of course, Christ himself had been a pacifist. The taking of life, therefore, is a sin, but it may be an admissible one if done to maintain peace, to protect innocents, or even to punish wrongdoers – but even here it must always be with the motive of ensuring peace.

Writing some 800 years later, fellow Christian theologian **Saint Thomas Aquinas** refined and formalized these approaches, so perhaps this is a good place to formally summarize the best-known form of just war theory. In his *Summa Theologica*, regarding justification *for* war (*jus ad bellum*, in legal Latin), Aquinas argues that wars should (1) be openly declared by a proper authority (e.g. governments, not private individuals); (2) have just cause (e.g. self-defence, not aggression); (3) be for the right purpose (e.g. to establish peace, not commercial gain); (4) be proportional (i.e. should not be an overreaction); and (5) be a last resort (all other means of resolution have failed). Regarding conduct *in* war (*jus in bello*), Aquinas adds two further criteria: he again stresses (1) proportionality (no excessive force should be used, just enough to achieve the objectives), and that (2) non-combatants should not be harmed.

A necessary evil

To some, of course, the idea of fighting for peace seems itself a contradiction – especially

The sons of Adam are limbs of each other,
Having been created of one essence.
When the calamity of time affects one limb
The other limbs cannot remain at rest.
If you have no sympathy for the troubles of others,
You are unworthy to be called by the name of a Human.

(Sa'adi (1210-92), Persian poet), translated by M–Aryanpour

United Nations emblem with poem found at entrance to UN building in New York

for a Christian pacifist. However, employing an argument that you'll by now recognize, both Augustine and Aquinas distinguished between what was permissible for the state, and what was allowed the individual citizen (where Christian ethics should still apply). Why did they not advocate pacifism? One answer may be that, during Augustine's lifetime, Christianity had risen to become the official religion of the Roman Empire – and empires tend not to flourish under pacifism. But was Christianity ever equipped to fulfil the role of state religion? In Jesus' advice to "Render therefore unto Caesar the

"The only excuse, therefore, for going to war is that we may live in peace unharmed."
Marcus Tullius Cicero

things which are Caesar's; and unto God the things that are God's" (Matthew 22:21), we may perhaps read an admission of this; that religion and state aim at different ends, and until the latter embodies the former, there can be no "just war".

Pacifism, of course, need not have a religious basis. The old maxim, sometimes attributed to Gandhi, "An eye for an eye will make the whole world blind", suggests the self-perpetuating futility of the never-ending cycle of conflict. But can states afford to "turn the other cheek"? Can they afford to sit back while innocents are slaughtered? Whether truly Christian or not, it was perhaps such considerations that influenced Aquinas and Augustine to concede that war was sometimes the lesser of two evils.

Blurry ethics

Even so, where just war criteria are met, and self-defence or the protection of innocents present a just cause, there are still problems. For instance, many consider World War II, and the fight against fascism, to have been a just war, but even this involved actions by the Allies that deliberately targeted civilians (e.g. the carpet-bombing of Dresden, Cologne and other German cities to break morale; the dropping of two atomic bombs on Japan, which some argue was primarily to demonstrate US military might). In other forms of warfare (such as recent conflicts in Afghanistan or Iraq, or the Vietnam War), the "enemy" is also not always clearly identifiable, blurring combatant and civilian, where guerrilla warfare and terrorism replace

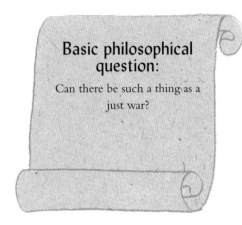

Basic philosophical question:

Can there be such a thing as a just war?

open conflict, taking place not on clearly delimited battle grounds but in among the streets and fields where ordinary people go about their daily lives. In such circumstances, it is almost inevitable that innocents will die – in fact, it's estimated that in modern warfare civilians now far outnumber military casualties.

An international social contract

These concerns aside, just war theory at least attempts to establish a set of criteria by which military action can be justified. As such, the theory forms the basis for modern approaches to war, informing the attempted role played by the United Nations in promoting security, preventing conflict and providing a forum for the resolution of international disputes. As **Thomas Hobbes** observed, while the social contract empowered the sovereign to keep citizens from dominating or terrorizing one another, there was no international equivalent. States were self-governing and had no automatic

"Where there is no common Power, there is no Law: where no Law, no Injustice. Force, and Fraud, are in warre the two Cardinall vertues."

Hobbes

obedience to one another or to any set of independent rules or guidelines. The UN may therefore perhaps be thought of as an attempt to redress the potential anarchy of this situation by developing a form of *international* social contract, the basis for a form of world government where its member countries are the "citizens".

The problem with this, however, is that the UN's powers seem limited. While Hobbes's sovereign had almost unlimited authority to ensure laws were upheld, the UN's international laws can be difficult to enforce. The UN Peacekeeping force is not sufficiently equipped to do so, which leaves any military or collective action subject to the agreement of its members. However, as the 2003 invasion of Iraq demonstrates, where a coalition of states led by the USA and UK grew impatient with Saddam Hussein's reluctance to comply with the UN Security Council resolutions regarding alleged possession of "weapons of mass destruction", individual countries may not always wait for permission before taking matters into their own hands. The UN may impose economic sanctions on problem states (as it did to help bring about the end of apartheid in South Africa in the 1980s), but these are subject to vote, and may even be vetoed by any one of its most powerful countries, thus undermining its democratic process. The UN may call out countries on its policies – "name and shame" those contravening human rights or other conventions – but this, while not ineffectual, still only amounts to "bad publicity" for the state in question.

Making a decision:

Just war theorists tend to see war as a necessary evil: to be avoided, if possible, but if not, to be conducted in a way that makes things better. What might you do to do that? Given the long history of trouble between your two countries, it seems that any new conflict is unlikely to resolve things. And, since the actions that have increased tensions are those of individuals, and are not state-sponsored, then there is no justification for revenge. It would be better to involve the international community – the UN, or some mutually agreed-upon independent arbitrator – and take Cicero's advice: talking comes first. Of course, some resent the idea of an unelected "world government" dominated by superpowers, but the arguments for its existence are as compelling at international as at national level.

It is rumoured that a hostile neighbouring state has developed nuclear weapons. Should I support my government in carrying out a pre-emptive strike?

Einstein • Russell • von Neumann • Morgenstern • Flood & Dresher • Nash • Kant

There continue to be problems with the state next door. Reports suggest that it is developing nuclear weapons. Given your fractious relationship, your government is getting worried. As you already possess nuclear arms, would the perceived threat justify "retaliating first"? Or should you wait and risk annihilation?

Though estimation is difficult, it's thought that at least 200,000 people died from the atomic bombs dropped on Hiroshima and Nagasaki, many from the initial blast, the rest from the effects of radiation over the following months and years. Long-term effects included leukaemia and other forms of cancer, and an increased incidence of birth defects in the offspring of survivors. The "Tsar" bomb, tested by the Soviet Union in 1961, was 1,500 times more powerful than the two Japanese explosions combined, and remains the most powerful weapon ever tested. Now, over 50 years later, it's estimated that the nuclear capacity of the USA alone is sufficient to destroy the world between five and fifty times over (depending on whom you believe – not that the difference matters!). Given that any significant nuclear conflict would be MAD (cause Mutually Assured Destruction), then you might wonder whether there's any need for having a nuclear arsenal: if you both know you'll never use it, what's the point in a deterrent that will never be employed, and therefore – arguably – does not in fact deter?

An international social contract

In 1939, concerned that the Germans were trying to develop nuclear weaponry, the German-born physicist **Albert Einstein** (1879–1955) wrote to President Franklin D Roosevelt, sparking the chain of events that eventually produced the Cold War arms race. Einstein merely wished to forestall any Nazi advantage – which, ironically, never occurred, leaving the pacifist Einstein with guilt at not only having prompted the development of the bomb, but also (through his discoveries in physics) enabled its conception. But this pacifism was not shared by other intellectuals, who argued that, if the world were to survive, then the power to destroy it should reside only with a single state.

Aside from contributions to logic and mathematics, the English philosopher

161

Bertrand Russell (1872–1970) is most commonly remembered as a campaigner for nuclear disarmament. But this had not always been his view. Jailed for pacifism during World War I, following America's development of nuclear weapons Russell became a vocal advocate for a pre-emptive strike against Russia. He was joined in this by the American **John von Neumann** (1903–57), a fellow mathematician and a pioneer of the computer, who had also worked on the development of the US atomic bomb (in the Manhattan Project). Both men argued that a pre-emptive strike, while Russia was yet to develop the bomb, would ensure long-term peace – better a winnable war now than a future conflict that could destroy the world. However, once the Soviets achieved nuclear parity, the game changed (perhaps one reason why Russell later abandoned this policy).

Game theory and nuclear war

The gaming metaphor here is not accidental. Von Neumann, together with American economist **Oskar Morgenstern** (1902–77),

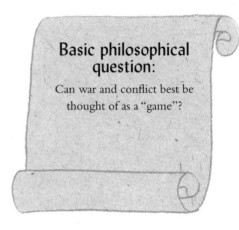

Basic philosophical question:

Can war and conflict best be thought of as a "game"?

had developed "game theory" as an application of mathematics to real-world situations, helping to devise the best strategy for various political and economic scenarios. Applied to nuclear war (and your dilemma), there is one game in particular that seems to provide a telling analysis. As detailed in William Poundstone's excellent 1992 book of the same name, the *Prisoner's Dilemma* has been hugely influential on modern economic, political and military strategy.

Prisoner A/ Prisoner B	Confess		Stay Silent	
Confess	2 years	2 years	3 years	0 years
Stay Silent	0 years	3 years	1 year	1 year

> *"I know not with what weapons World War III will be fought, but World War IV will be fought with sticks and stones."*
> Albert Einstein

Devised by **Merrill M Flood** (1908–91) and **Melvin Dresher** (1911–92), two mathematicians working on game theory for the RAND Corporation (an American global policy think tank), the game involves two players with four total potential outcomes. A typical illustration involves two people who are arrested together while engaged in some criminal activity. To prosecute, the police require at least one person to confess. Interviewed separately, with no means of conferring, the two are offered deals: inform on the other and go free, leaving the silent accomplice with three years in jail. However, if both remain silent, then, through lack of evidence, each gets only one year in jail. But, if both blab, then each gets two years.

A solution to this dilemma was proposed by American mathematician **John Nash** (1928–2015): whatever happens, the best strategy for each party, given the assumption that people act in their own self-interest, is to squeal. This is known as a "Nash equilibrium". Why, you will be wondering, doesn't Nash suggest that both prisoners stay silent? This is the problem that the prisoner's dilemma embodies: behaving in your own self-interest might provide the greatest gains (if you "sucker" the other person, as Poundstone puts it, who is trying to do the mutually beneficial thing), but if the other player also behaves selfishly, the gains are less than if you'd cooperated.

How does this apply to nuclear confrontation? The prisoner's dilemma is an example of what's called a *non-zero-sum game*: one player's loss is not always equalled by the other's gain, for there's an outcome in which both may cooperate to "win" (albeit not as much as if they'd "suckered" the other player). In this context, a war-like nation might consider the best strategy to be to attempt to gain dominance (building up their nuclear arsenal, identifying their opponent's weaknesses, in order to unleash a surprise attack). However, at times of great tension, this also risks MAD, and since nuclear arsenals are costly, it's not the ideal outcome for either nation. On the other hand, being without nuclear weapons, while better for peace and costs, would leave you vulnerable – and since each nation would seek to keep its military capacity secret, you might not know this until it was too late.

The ethical solution?

So what should you do? A Nash equilibrium suggests that, given the natural self-interest of both parties, the best thing is to possess nuclear weapons, which will leave you either in a position of dominance, or a tense but peaceful stalemate. And yet, if both players were more trusting, the even better outcome would surely be multilateral disarmament, allowing you to spend money on schools and hospitals, even maybe to develop closer peaceful ties with one another. It therefore comes down to trust – which, Nash suggests, is not the most "rational" strategy.

Nation A/ Nation B	Possess Nukes	Disarm
Possess Nukes	Uneasy peace Costly	Vulnerability/ annihilation — Dominance/victory
Disarm	Vulnerability/ annihilation — Dominance/victory	Less confrontational peace Frees resources for other things

But is it more rational to be selfish or selfless? The prisoner's dilemma may have no "solution". In contrast to Nash, philosophers such as **Immanuel Kant** would argue that cooperation and disarmament are the *only* truly moral options. Kant's answer to the prisoner's dilemma would therefore be to cooperate, based on the argument that there is a categorical imperative to treat others in the way we would want to be treated, to *universalize* our actions (*see* page 122); if we all follow this rule, then we live in a better world. But, as with other applications of morality to international politics, this risks being "naive". Kant's advice might give you the moral high ground, but Nash's would ensure you survived.

Making a decision:

While you might feel afraid at the implied threat of your neighbour's new nuclear capacity, it can help to realize that the reason it has developed nuclear weapons is because it feels threatened. Striking now would not only be fear-driven and irrational, but also – since you don't know its nuclear capacity – risk MAD. Assuming you both have nukes, the best strategy of all is not only not to use them, but to work toward multilateral disarmament.

Should I support my country if it decides to intervene in another country's domestic affairs?

Vidal • Chomsky • Orwell • Brzezinski • Mill • Lenin • Klein

Reports have surfaced of human rights atrocities committed in a developing country by a crazed despot. Certain factions in the press and in government are calling for your country to intervene in order to stop the chaos and slaughter. Should you support your government if it decides to do so?

For a state to be "democratic" is often considered a minimum requirement of civilization, and to be "undemocratic" as synonymous with totalitarianism or barbarism. Modern democracy is idealistically viewed as the social embodiment of equality, granting freedom of thought and action, civil liberties and human rights. If a Western power intervenes in some foreign conflict, justification is therefore often couched in terms of promoting these values, "liberating" people "oppressed" by "despotic tyrants". I put "scare quotes" around these words not because I think that such terms are always relative – there certainly exist such oppressive regimes and despotic tyrants – but because the motives for foreign intervention are often clouded by other, less "noble" concerns.

Doublethink

Critics of the First (1990–91) and Second Iraq Wars (2003–11) and the War in Afghanistan (2001–) have observed how neatly the various pretexts for invasion coincided with the Western powers' economic need to control the region's oil supply. Some have also seen the "War on Terror" as (in part, at least) a pretext for beefing up state security and surveillance at home. Observing this alleged tendency of modern states to mask imperial intentions with democratic language, **Gore Vidal** noted that, "Words are used to disguise, not to illuminate, action: you liberate a city by destroying it." Similarly, **Noam Chomsky** observes that aggressive military actions are often defended in such a way: "I have never heard of a state that admits it's carrying out an aggressive act, they're always engaged in 'defense,' no matter what they're doing – maybe 'preemptive defense' or something." The fact that no such weapons of mass destruction (WMDs) were ever found in Iraq, or firm evidence for Iraqi leader Saddam Hussein's sponsorship of terrorism (another pretext put forward), perhaps suggests that the conflict never really depended on their existence.

The above examples are illustrations of Orwellian "doublethink". In **George Orwell**'s *Nineteen Eighty-Four* (1949), the totalitarian society ruled by Big Brother justifies its oppressive policies by employing words in their opposite sense. Thus, the three slogans of the Party – "WAR IS PEACE. FREEDOM IS SLAVERY.

IGNORANCE IS STRENGTH" – imply that traditional values are actually weaknesses. War is obviously not peace, but it is justifiable because it involves *fighting for* peace; therefore, to permanently ensure peace we must make constant war. The "freedom" to do what you want is to be enslaved by misleading desires (Plato would have agreed), and to be "enslaved" by Big Brother's rules is actually to be "liberated". And *not* to know things – where those things are "wrong" – is actually a positive virtue. Underlying doublethink is therefore an authoritarian concern with *autonomy*: the populace, lacking self-control and rationality, ignorant of what's good for it, must be manipulated and controlled by disguised language. For Vidal and Chomsky, such language is either short-sighted hypocrisy or else a deliberate smokescreen for foreign policy – a democratic veil over imperialist authoritarianism that – in some ways – makes America no less an empire than that of Britain in the time of the Raj.

In support of the "Great Game"

But, while there might be a need to disguise it, not everyone views such imperialism negatively. **Zbigniew Brzezinski** (1928–2017), a Polish-American political scientist who served in various capacities under two US presidents, admitted that "Democracy is inimical to imperial mobilization", but nonetheless saw the job of the foreign policy as extending global influence, through military dominance or political cooperation: "the three grand imperatives of imperial geostrategy are to prevent collusion and maintain security

> **Basic philosophical question:**
> Is the age of empire gone, or has empire simply been reinvented?

dependence among the vassals, to keep tributaries pliant and protected, and to keep the barbarians from coming together". Of course, this might be for ultimately worthy ends, but – as the language of describing smaller countries as "vassals", "tributaries" and "barbarians" implies – the suggested means were not always those of open diplomacy. For instance, before the Soviet invasion of Afghanistan, Brzezinski advised covert support for the Afghan Mujahideen, an Islamic guerrilla military group, which Brzezinski hoped to use to bog down Russian forces in a draining war of attrition – a ploy that succeeded. But in arming and supporting one faction against another for strategic ends, the players in this geopolitical "game" have often ignored or not foreseen the effects of such policies, failing to consider the agendas of the factions in question. When asked, years later, whether he regretted fuelling Islamic militantism, Brzezinski replied, "What was more important to the history of the world? ... Some stirred-up Muslims or the liberation of

central Europe and the end of the Cold War?" Of course, the US is not alone in playing the Great Game (as geopolitics was called in the 19th century), and similar examples could be drawn from the recent history of many states.

"The West knows best"

But what gives states the *right* to intervene and manipulate? Like Hobbes, Brzezinski and his ilk are "realists", justifying the game of global dominance by the vacuum that exists in international governance – assuming, in fact, that it's the *duty* of some superpower or group of nations to fill that vacuum, to "educate" the rest of the world as to the good of democracy, liberalism and fast food. This "paternalist" approach in fact can be found in **John Stuart Mill**, who declared that "despotism is a legitimate mode of government in dealing with barbarians, provided the end be their improvement". The spread of English language and culture,

political values and economic practice, was therefore a right and proper thing. Behind imperialism old and new, the idea still seems to be that "the West knows best".

The other incentive for imperialism is, of course, capitalism. As Russian communist revolutionary **Vladimir Lenin** (1870–1924) argued, because "modern monopolist capitalism" takes place "on a world-wide scale", "imperialist wars are absolutely inevitable under such an economic system, as long as private property in the means of production exists". Colonialism develops once the home markets fail to yield the profits required for further economic growth, which generates geopolitical conflict, as colonial powers fight over the exploitation of weaker nations' resources. And for these reasons, Lenin considered World War I to be merely another conflict in the Great Game – a geopolitical squabble over the division of spoils – after which, regardless of who won, the working classes would continue to be exploited.

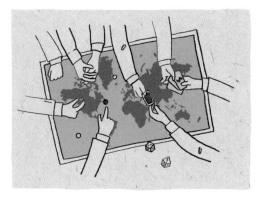

Disaster capitalism

This marriage of geopolitics and capitalism reaches its most cynical modern expression in what is called "disaster capitalism". Canadian writer **Naomi Klein** argues that not only do multinational corporations and economic organizations benefit from disasters, but they deliberately employ them to enforce economic and social change. Klein cites the transformation of the Chilean economy following the military coup led by General Pinochet, the "liberalization" of post-Soviet Russia and the 2003 Iraq War – which, she

claims, combined military and corporate ends, to go farthest in employing economic "shock therapy": "using moments of collective trauma to engage in radical social and economic engineering".

Even natural disasters can provide opportunities for disaster capitalism, as private companies capitalize on disruption to state services and infrastructure to establish profit-making enterprises. Following the Sri Lankan tsunami in 2004, from which a quarter of a million people died and a further 2.5 million were made homeless, "foreign investors and international lenders had teamed up to use the atmosphere of panic to hand the entire beautiful coastline over to entrepreneurs who quickly built large resorts, blocking hundreds of thousands of fishing people from rebuilding their villages near the water". Similar things happened after Hurricane Katrina. Thus, even the international rush to provide philanthropic aid may not always be what it seems.

Making a decision:

Given the geopolitical motives of any power capable of intervening in foreign wars or atrocities, it's probably wise to question their motives. Capitalism and geopolitical change – whether natural or man-made – can go hand in hand. While such enterprises may look and think of themselves differently, are they any different from the empires of old? In many cases, it's been the behind-the-scenes game playing of Western powers that created such problems in the first place. Long term, the United Nations' role in strengthening international law and fostering human rights and democracy seems to present the best solution.

A new political party promises "progressive change". Can I believe that it can offer anything new?

Fukuyama • Marx • Hegel • Gray

A new political party arises, denouncing the "tired old policies" of established rivals, and promising "a fair and just society". Their slogans engage the youth, gaining popular support, but though their ideas appeal, you've seen it all before. Does anything ever really change? Is progress an illusion?

The 20th century was dominated by two opposing ideologies: liberal democracy and communism. Both promised progress: one toward increased standards of living, freedom of opportunity and personal wealth; the other toward greater equality, freedom from exploitation and communal plenty. At the fall of the Berlin Wall in 1989, and with it the demise of the Soviet Union, capitalism's proponents crowed for victory. American political economist **Francis Fukuyama** (b. 1952) went even further, declaring "the end of history": "That is, the end point of mankind's ideological evolution and the universalization of Western liberal democracy as the final form of human government" (*The End of History and the Last Man*, 1992).

It will all work out in the end...
Subsequent developments suggest Fukuyama's bold claim was somewhat premature. For while it's true that, in most instances, communism led to authoritarian oppression and poverty; and also true that capitalism (the driving force of liberal democracy) has increased standards of living

and general wealth, creating more egalitarian and open societies, this victory has come at a cost. Since Fukuyama's proclamation, there has been a steady procession of financial crises, culminating in a global recession (of which we are still in the shadow), an increasing gap between rich and poor, and yet more signs – if any were needed – that climate change is real. And yet capitalism seems ill equipped to deal with these problems, for many proposed solutions – favouring stability over risk, fostering social equality, concern for the environment – are not strictly dictated by profit. Add to this the negative effects of globalization, as wealthy economies exploit the cheap labour and resources of the developing world, and the practice of "disaster capitalism" (highlighted by Naomi Klein), and unfettered capitalism begins to look less like the answer and more like the problem.

Capitalism's defenders see these as teething problems – we must be patient. Eventually, free-market capitalism and liberal democracy will work. Of course, the advocates of communism pleaded similar excuses: we must have faith in eventual progress. But what if the question here is not *which* ideology to have faith in, but whether we should believe in ideologies at *all*?

Faith in progress

Karl Marx's ideal of a communist society was seen as the culmination of an inevitable historical process (*see* page 39). Having exhausted itself, capitalism would leave the ideal conditions for the introduction of a *dictatorship of the proletariat*, a temporary workers' state that would gradually wither away, leaving a perfectly equal society. Marx's notion of this process – what is termed *dialectical materialism* – was based on the philosophy of **Georg Wilhelm Friedrich Hegel**. However, where Marx's vision was atheistic and materialist, Hegel's was religious and spiritual. For Hegel, it was the inevitable

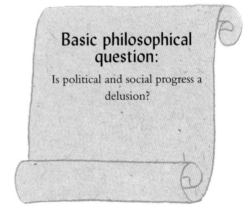

Basic philosophical question:

Is political and social progress a delusion?

evolution of ideas that would usher in the final stages of historical development – complete "self-consciousness" – where humanity would realize itself as *Absolute Spirit* (God). History was therefore a means by which God comes to realize Himself. In

Evolution has no end goal. If humans are just animals, then does human history have no destination?

I'm waiting for...

Hegel
The realization of the Absolute Spirit

Christianity
The Day of Judgment

Transhumanism
The Singularity

Marx
Global communism

owing its structure to Hegel, Marxism may therefore be thought of as a form of secular religion, its progress toward its end-goal no less a matter of faith.

But, even if true, does this make *all* belief in progress "religious" in nature? The English philosopher **John Gray** (b. 1948) thinks so: "To believe in progress is to believe that,

by using the new powers given to us by growing scientific knowledge, humans can free themselves from the limits that frame the lives of other animals" (*Straw Dogs*, 2002). But, no less products of evolution, human rationality, moral goodness and free will are as much matters of "faith" as the tenets of any religion (and therefore, for

> *"[T]he utopian faith in a condition of future harmony is a Christian inheritance, and so is the modern idea of progress."*
> John Gray

Gray, baseless). As evidence, Gray points to *transhumanism* (the doctrine that humans can evolve "beyond" current limitations using technology) as an indication that even scientists are not immune to the old religious dreams of immortality, godlike knowledge and omnipotence. This will be enabled by the *Singularity*, when machine intelligence reaches a sort of critical mass, enabling computers to design better versions of themselves.

A futile delusion

Evolution, Gray points out, is not something we can take control of, for even as we think we do, we merely express those very urges that evolution has bred in us. And evolution itself, of course, does not develop "better" or "higher" qualities, merely those that have proven most adequate for ensuring survival. The idea that we can somehow exempt ourselves from this process is therefore a fundamentally Christian one: we are *not like* other animals; we are *different*.

Gray's view is bleak, taking aim at general notions of progress, secular and religious alike, and – for whatever reasons – many may not wish to follow him to its conclusions. However, his critique of human ambitions for a better world (whatever form that would take) asks some awkward questions – for both socialism and capitalism. At the very least it suggests we rethink what we consider possible, and what our goals should be.

Making a decision:

Experience may have taught you to be sceptical of promises of social progress. However, perhaps it's true that (for some, at least, and in certain respects) life is better than it used to be. Human beings generally live longer, have better standards of healthcare, know and can accomplish more through technology and science. We may also point to social improvements – greater sexual and racial equality, broader acceptance of human rights. Even if we are no more than animals, and cannot escape our mortality, might we not agree and work toward more modest measures of progress?

Should I have children?

Malthus • Kant • Parfit

Given the state of the world, you may sometimes ask yourself whether it would be better not to bring children into it – wouldn't that be an injustice to them? Or, at least, with growing concerns over climate change and overpopulation, don't you owe it to future generations to ensure a better life for them?

At the beginning of the 19th century, the global population was around 1 billion. Since then, it has increased sevenfold, and the United Nations Population Division estimates that it will pass 10 billion sometime during the 2050s. By that time, with advancements in medicine and technology – assuming they have access to it – people will also be capable of living even longer. Unless climate change is reversed, this will also coincide with rising sea levels, with increased flooding and loss of land; reduced crop yields, due to rise in global temperature and fluctuating weather patterns; a reduced amount of fresh water, leading to drought, famine and disease – and so on (I don't want to depress you). All of this may not be inevitable, but with prominent advocates of the interests of big business also favouring "climate change denial", you may be forgiven for your lack of optimism.

Natural limits

Of course, you may take the view that such disasters as occur from the failure of human beings to live in balance with their environment are merely nature's way of maintaining that balance. This was the view of the English economist **Thomas Robert Malthus** (1766–1834), who argued that,

unless kept in check, population tends to exhaust its resources. As he put it: "The perpetual tendency of the race of man to increase beyond the means of subsistence is one of the general laws of animated nature, which we can have no reason to expect to change" (*Essay on the Principle of Population*, 1798). And what happens when population approaches its limits of sustainability? Malthus argues that a series of "checks" – disease, famine, war, natural disasters and so forth – restore the population to manageable size.

But can't we intervene to prevent such catastrophes? Malthus thought not: "To prevent the recurrence of misery is, alas! beyond the power of man." The problem is, he thought, that while population increases in "geometrical ratio" – an exponential curve, doubling its output with each generation (think of rabbits in springtime…) – resources increase only in "arithmetical ratio" (a steady constant rise). Of course, we might try to curb reproduction – such as China's "one child policy" attempted between 1979 and 2015 – but, apart from being difficult to enforce (especially in liberal countries), the main foe is nature itself – the human urge to reproduce.

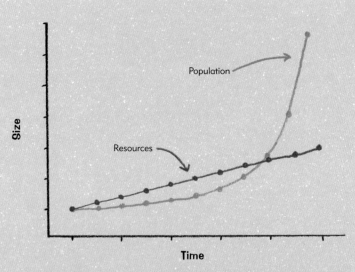

Even where a society's resources continue to increase, its growth can only be steady (*arithmetical progression*). In contrast, population starts slowly, but increases *exponentially*, eventually far outstripping a society's ability to support it.

Hypothetical persons

And yet, we have to do *something*, surely? What about our duty to future generations? But some philosophers have questioned whether, morally, we have one. The issue here is the concept of a "future person". If we take the sort of duty ethics outlined by **Immanuel Kant** (*see* page 124), then we can see that the moral community includes only *current* persons, not *hypothetical* ones. If my irresponsible behaviour deprives you of some good that you have a right to expect (food, security, etc.), then it may be considered immoral; but if my use of common resources does not currently injure or deprive any currently existing person, then – regardless of what consequences this has for future generations – my behaviour is *not* immoral. (We'll ignore for now the question of whether such behaviour *does* in fact impact

on current people, which we'll return to when we consider global poverty.)

But, as was noted earlier, Kant does not permit us to be cruel or wasteful regarding animals and nature; although trees and dogs are not persons, we have, he says, a duty not to treat other organisms irresponsibly or callously, for such behaviour may breed bad moral habits *in us*. Could such an approach form the basis of concern for the environment or future generations? Some philosophers think it can, because, while we might not be able to think of this as a *direct* or "perfect" duty (as Kant terms it), it can form part of our indirect, "imperfect" duty to improve our *own* moral nature. In other words, being "environmentally ethical" would make us better moral persons. Furthermore, we might limit population on the grounds that it would affect the

174

environment and natural resources, which would in turn affect our duties to those who already exist.

The utilitarian perspective

However, others argue that, viewed from a utilitarian/consequentialist perspective, our duties to the environment and future people are not so clear. In *Reasons and Persons* (1984), the English philosopher **Derek Parfit** (1942–2017) presents what he terms "the repugnant conclusion". Consider the total positive life experience for a population – what makes life worth living. Now, if we assume that a population of a certain size has a certain total positive life experience, we can always imagine a situation where adding more people will increase this total. Compared to before, the additional people

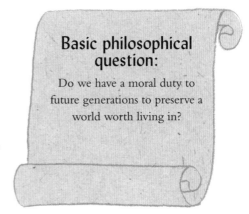

Basic philosophical question:

Do we have a moral duty to future generations to preserve a world worth living in?

may have a *lesser* (but still positive) quality of life, but the overall calculation shows that the total is greater.

Let's take a simple example: there are two of you sharing a pizza, when there's a knock at the door, and two of your friends show

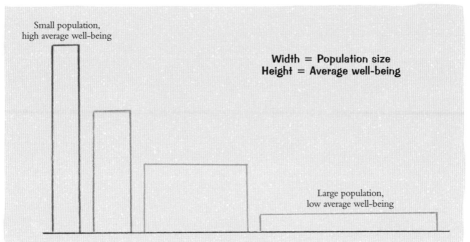

Small population, high average well-being

Width = Population size
Height = Average well-being

Large population, low average well-being

The Repugnant Conclusion: For a population with a certain positive quality of life, we can always imagine a greater one with less (but still positive) quality of life.

> *"For any possible population of at least ten billion people, all with a very high quality of life, there must be some much larger imaginable population whose existence, if other things are equal, would be better even though its members have lives that are barely worth living."*
>
> Derek Parfit

up. Being a good host, you offer them an equal share of your food. This makes you all not as happy or contented as when only two of you were sharing, but it is still a positive experience – it's better than having *no* pizza (a negative experience, if you're hungry), and we may argue that it is better that more people have *some* pizza (some positive experience) than fewer. Parfit's argument is therefore roughly equivalent to saying that no matter how many people turn up for pizza – *as long as their overall experience is still positive* – then you are still not entitled to turn people away, for it is the overall happiness of the group that counts (and, given enough people, all those barely positive experiences will add up).

Applying Parfit's argument to the environment or to the decision of whether to have children, we can see what's "repugnant" about it, for it suggests that we are morally entitled to carry on being selfish and wasteful, reducing the future quality of life of people yet unborn to minimal (though still – *barely* – positive) levels.

Making a decision:

It's difficult to think about future people. From a Kantian perspective, it may be possible to argue that we are indirectly responsible for ensuring a better world, which may lead you to question adding people to it. However, like many people, you may think such considerations outweighed by short-term positive happiness (you can still be environmentally responsible and a parent – for now, at least). You may think that Malthus is wrong, and that science will find a solution to both climate change and overpopulation. Parfit's repugnant conclusion may therefore seem a distant scenario that needn't concern you. Or maybe you're in fact an illustration of his point: there are more people on the planet now than ever – but are you happier than previous generations?

Should I give to charity?

Nozick • Kant • Hayek • Rawls • Pogge • Pilger • Singer

Their agents stop you as you walk through the shopping centre, or even turn up on your doorstep. You receive their unsolicited mail and phone calls, and see their causes promoted through TV, newspaper and internet adverts. You feel bad, of course, walking past them, turning them away or switching channel, but what can you do? You're not rich, and if you gave to every deserving case you'd be as poor as the people they're trying to help.

And is charity even the answer? You've heard that half of it goes on bureaucracy or gets pocketed by corrupt middlemen. And isn't it the government's job to sort such things out? Or the United Nations'? I mean, it's not as if *you've* caused these problems – is it?

The above, or something similar, has probably passed through most people's minds at one time or another. Aside from the logistical question of the best way to help, the main philosophical issue underlying charity giving is whether we are morally obliged to aid those worse off than us – would it be *unjust* not to?

Imperfect duties

If we take broad concerns like poverty, then some will argue that there is no direct moral duty, because an unequal division of property and wealth is simply a consequence of the way the world is. So, for instance, **Robert Nozick** would argue that there should be no enforced redistribution of wealth or taxation to alleviate inequality and poverty because – unless it can be shown that some injustice has taken place (as outlined in his *entitlement*

theory, see page 129) – this would restrict freedom. Of course, we may still feel morally obliged to do something, because a good person will naturally desire to help someone who is suffering. However, such obligations need not take a definite form – they are, as **Immanuel Kant** would say, *imperfect* duties: we should help others, but it's up to us as to when, how and to what degree. So, you might walk past the person begging on the corner, but make a charity donation at your place of work.

Friedrich Hayek reinforces Nozick's point from an economic perspective. If we redistribute wealth or regulate the market in an attempt to alleviate poverty or injustice, then we also interfere with the *extended order* (the natural relations of supply and demand, price, etc., arising from the free interaction of individuals). This will make the market unstable, erratic and difficult to predict, thus undermining the benefits of free trade. This may be a fair point – if we assume Hayek's ideal of a free market. In practice, however, the "extended order" that Hayek defends does not actually exist, because markets are arguably already skewed by corruption, monopolies, price fixing, one-sided trade agreements and other factors. Shouldn't our duty therefore be to put people before markets?

Global responsibilities...

As we've seen, **John Rawls** argues that some redistribution of wealth is necessary in order to create a just society. Without it – whether those individuals who possess greater wealth are "entitled" to it or not – certain individuals may be denied access to basic primary goods, losing out in education or jobs, quality of life and so on. In terms of our own community, then, Rawls would argue that helping those in need must take *at least* some institutional and legal form – we can't just leave it up to the charitable inclinations of well-meaning individuals.

The German philosopher **Thomas Pogge** (b. 1953) would go even further. Shouldn't Rawls's principles of justice be applied not just *within* a society, but *globally*? Pogge argues that many lesser-developed countries find themselves in poverty not as a consequence of bad luck, acts of God or their own bad management, but through the deliberate policies of rich states, who have colonized, exploited and manipulated those countries to their own ends. These inequalities are now enshrined in conventions and trade deals, in debt obligations and other agreements that maintain these inequalities. For instance, in *The New Rulers of the World* (2001), the Australian journalist **John Pilger** (b. 1939) details how, following a brutal military

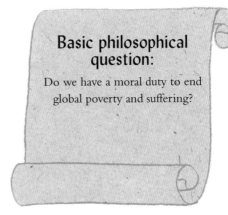

Basic philosophical question:

Do we have a moral duty to end global poverty and suffering?

coup in 1968, Indonesia opened to foreign investment, becoming – according to the World Bank – a "model pupil", ready to learn the lessons of free-market capitalism (an example of "disaster capitalism"). "Within a year of the bloodbath," he points out, "Indonesia's economy was effectively redesigned in America, giving the West access to vast mineral wealth, markets and cheap labour." In a country where over a quarter of people live in poverty, this meant the proliferation of sweatshops, where, amid oppressive, dangerous and unsanitary conditions, men, women and children worked long shifts for pitiful wages.

So, while there is a general perception that poverty in such countries as Indonesia exists because of some factor internal to the country itself, the truth is that the West has often been complicit in creating that situation. As Pogge observes, "If we offer a prize, so to speak, to anyone who manages to bring a country under his physical control – namely, that they can then sell the

> *"When we buy new clothes not to keep ourselves warm but to look 'well-dressed' we are not providing for any important need. We would not be sacrificing anything significant if we were to continue to wear our old clothes, and give the money to famine relief. By doing so, we would be preventing another person from starving."*
> Peter Singer

country's resources and borrow in its name – then it's not surprising that generals or guerrilla movements will want to compete for this prize. But that the prize is there is really not the fault of the insiders. It is the fault of the dominant states and of the system of international law they maintain."

...Global duties

What then is the answer? "Clearly," Pogge argues, "we could eradicate severe global poverty – through a reform of the global order or through other initiatives designed to compensate for its effects on the global poor" ("'Assisting' the Global Poor", 2003) – and all without lessening the West's own quality

of life. In fact, he argues, it would require a relatively minor redistribution. The only barrier is the general assumption that it is not "our" fault.

Peter Singer makes a similar argument ("Famine, Affluence, and Morality", 1971). Regardless of what causes such suffering, or what the best way to help is, the moral argument is simple: if people are starving, destitute or dying from preventable or curable diseases, and we can do something about it, then we should. Singer's famous illustration is of a child drowning in a shallow pond: if you were passing, wouldn't you wade in to save it? The cost to you is negligible (perhaps it will ruin your clothes),

Thomas Pogge

Robert Nozick

It would be easy to sacrifice one trip to the cinema and instead donate the money to charity

but the benefit (saving a life) is immeasurably greater. Accordingly, we should donate all we can to charity (our complete disposable income), foregoing all luxuries, for – in utilitarian terms – how can a visit to the cinema, or a meal at a restaurant, outweigh a human life?

Singer's case is emotionally and rationally compelling, but it does ask a lot of people.

Also, while he is not unaware of the type of points made by Pogge regarding the role played by free-market capitalism and Western governments, he still argues that our main focus should be our own personal responsibility – for any action now, even if less effective, is better than waiting for political change while people die and suffer.

Making a decision:

While it is a personal decision, and you may feel that your contribution makes little difference, there are still good reasons to give to charity. If Pilger and Pogge are correct, then the global economic order is largely responsible for a great deal of poverty and suffering in developing countries, and we should both seek to change and redress the effects of that. In the meantime, as Singer argues, much individual good can be done to alleviate the conditions of those worse off than us, for every little counts.

Why does Hollywood think the future is so grim?

Gray • Aristotle • More • Bacon • Bregman • Marx • Plato • Kant

Sometimes, while watching yet another cinematic depiction of a dystopian future, you may have cause for despair. You may allow your mind to wander: might we not, one day, through technology and social progress, build a brighter, better future, a world of peace and plenty, harmony and justice, where corruption, greed and human stupidity have all been banished to the waste bin of history? – only to be brought crashing back to earth by the all too credible worry that human nature might turn such dreams into some new and equally horrible dystopia. Given our history, you may therefore wonder whether *all* political systems are flawed, or whether it is *we* who are the problem. Are we, as **John Gray** argues, fundamentally irrational beings who cannot hope ever to live in a completely just society? Or, as **Aristotle** and others have argued, are human beings fundamentally good, requiring merely the right type of leadership and political organization to flourish? Should we lower our sights, or raise them?

Utopias and dystopias

The word "utopia" itself was coined by the English statesman **Thomas More** (1478–1535) in his work by that name (1516), in which he pictured an island community living in harmony according to monastic-type laws. The English lawyer and philosopher Sir **Francis Bacon** (1561–26) also pictured an island in his *New Atlantis* (1627), a progressive society run by scientist–philosophers. As well as religious and scientific utopias, modern political ideologies have also had their utopian advocates: *Looking Backward: 2000 to 1887*, a huge bestseller in its day, was an 1888 novel by the American journalist Edward Bellamy (1850–98), telling

> "*Kindness and good nature unite men more effectually and with greater strength than any agreements whatsoever, since thereby the engagements of men's hearts become stronger than the bond and obligation of words.*"
> Thomas More

of a future American socialist utopia; while *The Dispossessed* (1974), by the American sci-fi and fantasy author Ursula Le Guin (b. 1929), presents the virtues of a utopian anarchist planet.

However, literary history contains far more *dystopias* than utopias – too many to mention. In fact, as a genre, modern sci-fi may be said to be largely dystopic. Does this suggest that utopian ideals are unrealistic, or merely less narratively interesting? It's hard to say.

In *Utopia for Realists* (2017), Dutch historian **Rutger Bregman** (b. 1988) argues that a utopian society need not be fantasy. In fact, the problem with contemporary socialist politics, he says, is that they are not utopian *enough*. Among his suggestions, Bregman argues for a universal basic income: if robots and automation are eventually to take away all gainful employment, then society must support people. Accordingly, Bregman argues for a standard 15-hour working week, where we are all paid for working less. I don't know about you, but I'm on board already.

Just as the alchemical search for gold laid the foundation for chemistry, the search for the perfect society has driven political change.

> ## Basic philosophical question:
> Is humanity ungovernable? Should we stop dreaming of the perfect society?

Useful dreams

But what would we do with so much free time? Wouldn't we get bored? Don't we need work in order to give our lives purpose? Arguably not, Bregman says, especially when so many modern jobs are meaningless and dispiriting. Why shouldn't we be paid to be creative or to follow humanitarian goals instead? Or simply to pursue leisure? Freed from work, there would be lots to do. **Karl Marx** would not have disagreed, for while he argued that we are essentially "productive" beings (*see* page 40), this need not take the form of meaningful work (in the current sense).

It's easy to poke holes in Bregman's ideas, but perhaps the dream of a utopian society is important in the same way as the alchemists' dream of turning lead into gold was: in the process of chasing what was ultimately a delusion, modern chemistry was born. And so, in political science, the dream of the perfect society has driven – and still does drive – progress towards greater fairness, equality and

justice. In this sense, while **Plato's** political views have been subject to extensive criticism, his *Republic* continues to be one of the most influential political texts ever written, having spurred countless subsequent thinkers and writers to improve or better it.

As for whether people are inherently ungovernable, we may consider the words of **Immanuel Kant:** "out of wood so crooked and perverse as that which man is made of, nothing absolutely straight can ever be wrought" ("Idea for a General History with a Cosmopolitan Purpose", 1784). Kant is not here suggesting that humans are inherently incorrigible, but merely that, as a ruler, it does not pay to be perfectionist: one can only try one's best. Ultimately, it is the individual's choice that determines whether he or she behaves justly – in accordance with the moral law – or not. Perhaps, then, political guidance, while necessary, is insufficient, for no matter how perfect a society is, it is only as good as each individual citizen's free choice.

Making a decision:

Some of history's most noble utopian dreams have turned out to be dystopian nightmares, but it may be argued that what political and social progress we have made is owed to such striving. It is likely, in fact, that such ambitions represent shifting goals, things that motivate us to improve, without actually presenting any real possibility of being fulfilled. Of course, in another sense, the opposite is also true: the distant visions of past generations – political, technological – are now mundane; we live in their dreamed-of future, and our future dreams have moved on. Before you collapse in despair at the dystopian horrors that surround you, perhaps you should consider how far we have come.

Bibliography

List of sources quoted from/alluded to:

Chapter 1:

My car has just been stolen! But can I hold the thieves responsible?
Jean-Paul Sartre, *Existentialism and Humanism* [1946]; trans. Philip Mairet (Methuen, 1989)
Thomas Hobbes, *Leviathan* (1651)

My friend says that I'm getting too fat. But, surely, it's none of her business?
Niccolò Machiavelli, *The Prince* [1532]; trans. W K Marriott (J M Dent & Co., 1908)
John Stuart Mill, *On Liberty* (1859)
Aristotle, *Nicomachean Ethics* [350 BCE]; trans. Harris Rackham (Harvard University Press, 1934)

Should I watch what I say on Twitter?
John Stuart Mill, *On Liberty* (1859)
United Nations, *Universal Declaration of Human Rights* (1948)
Joel Feinberg, *Offense to Others* (Oxford University Press, 1985)
Glenn Greenwald, "The Noxious Fruits of Hate Speech Laws" ww.Salon.com (2008), http://www.salon.com/2008/01/13 /hate_speech_laws/ (accessed 15 September 2017)

Is it OK to be addicted to Facebook?
Isaiah Berlin, "Two Concepts of Liberty" [1958], *Liberty* (Oxford University Press, 2002)
Plato, *The Republic* [c. 380 BCE]; trans. Benjamin Jowett (Clarendon Press, 1888)
Immanuel Kant, *Groundwork of the Metaphysics of Morals* [1785]; trans. Mary Gregor (Cambridge University Press, 2012)

Do I really have to wear a bicycle helmet?
Aristotle, *Politics* [350 BCE]; trans. Benjamin Jowett (Clarendon Press, 1885)
G W F Hegel, *Philosophy of Right* [1820]; trans. S W Dyde (G Bell & Sons, 1896)
John Stuart Mill, *On Liberty* (1859)

If I believe that eating meat is wrong, shouldn't everyone else?
John Rawls, "Kantian Constructivism in Moral Theory" [1980], in *Collected Papers*, ed. S Freeman (Harvard University Press, 1999)
Isaiah Berlin, "My Intellectual Path", in *The Power of Ideas* (Princeton University Press, 2000)
Will Kymlicka, *Contemporary Political Philosophy: An Introduction* (Oxford University Press, 1990)
Will Kymlicka, *Multicultural Citizenship: A Liberal Theory of Minority Rights* (Oxford University Press, 1996)

Is it wrong to want a bigger house?
Emily Badger, "How the Housing Crisis Left us More Racially Segregated", *The Washington Post* (2015) https://www.washingtonpost.com/news/wonk/wp/2015/05/08/how-the-housing-crisis-left-us-more-racially-segregated/?utm_term=.da8b99c8f24f (accessed 15 September 2017)
Adam Smith, *The Wealth of Nations* (1776)
Noam Chomsky, *Understanding Power* (Vintage, 2002)

Wall Street, dir. Oliver Stone (Twentieth Century Fox, 1987)
Ferdinand Mount, *The New Few* (Simon & Schuster, 2012)
Roberto A. Ferdman, "The Pay Gap Between CEOs and Workers Is Much Worse Than You Realize", *The Washington Post* (2014) https://www.washingtonpost.com/news/wonk/wp/2014/09/25/the-pay-gap-between-ceos-and-workers-is-much-worse-than-you-realize/?utm_term=.09e0db4415f9 (accessed 15 September 2017)

I've just lost my job to a robot! What can I do?
Martin Ford, *Rise of the Robots* (Oneworld Publications, 2015)
Karl Marx, "Critique of the Gotha Programme" [1875] (Foreign Languages Press, 1972)
Karl Marx and Friedrich Engels, *The German Ideology* [1845] (Lawrence & Wishart, 1970)
Karl Marx, "Fragment on Machines", *Grundrisse* (1857–61)

Chapter 2:

Is my local golf club a fair society?
George Orwell, *Animal Farm* [1945] (Penguin Classics, 2000)
John Rawls, *A Theory of Justice* (Harvard University Press, 1971)
John C. Harsanyi, "Can the Maximin Principle Serve as a Basis for Morality?", *American Political Science Review*, vol. 69, no. 2 (June 1975)
Michael J. Sandel, *Liberalism and the Limits of Justice* (Cambridge University Press, 1982)
Alasdair MacIntyre, *After Virtue* (Duckworth, 1981)
"The Day of the Doctor", *Doctor Who*, BBC (23 November 2013)

Should I bother to vote?
Daniel S. Levine, "Over 90 Million Eligible Voters Didn't Vote in the 2016 Presidential Election", www.Heavy.com (2017) http://heavy.com/news/2016/11/eligible-voter-turnout-for-2016-data-hillary-clinton-donald-trump-republican-democrat-popular-vote-registered-results/ (accessed 15 September 2017)
Barney Henderson, "Huge Turnout of 72.2 Per Cent for EU Referendum with 33.6 Million Voting", *The Telegraph* (2016) http://www.telegraph.co.uk /news/2016/06/23/high-turnout-for-eu-referendum -vote-could-break-uk-records/ (accessed 15 September 2017)
Henry Samuel, "French Election: Macron Secures Absolute Parliamentary Majority Amid Record Low Turnout", *The Telegraph* (2017) http://www.telegraph.co.uk/news/2017/06/18/french-election-macron-track-massive -parliamentary-majority/ (accessed 15 September 2017)
John Stuart Mill, *Considerations on Representative Government* (1861)
Gore Vidal, *The Decline and Fall of the American Empire* (Odonian Press, 1992)
Judith Burns, "Almost a Third of MPs Went to Private School", www.bbc.co.uk (2015) http://www.bbc.co.uk/news/education-32692789 (accessed 15 September 2017)
Friedrich Nietzsche, *Twilight of the Idols* [1889]; trans. A M Ludovici (Macmillan, 1911)
Plato, *The Republic* [c. 380 BCE]; trans. Benjamin Jowett (Clarendon Press, 1888)
John Stuart Mill, *On Liberty* (1859)

Bibliography

Sir Winston Churchill, House of Commons Debate (11 November 1947), vol. 444, col. 207

Noam Chomsky and Edward S Herman, *Manufacturing Consent* (Vintage, 1988)

How should we decide what to watch on TV?
Jeremy Bentham, *The Rationale of Reward* (1825)
Jeremy Bentham, "Commonplace Book", *Collected Works*, vol. 10 (William Tait, 1843)
Jeremy Bentham, "Anarchical Fallacies", *Collected Works*, vol. 2 (William Tait, 1843)
John Locke, *Essay Concerning Human Understanding* (1689)
John Stuart Mill, *Utilitarianism* (1861)
Karl Popper, *The Open Society and its Enemies* (Princeton University Press, 1952)
R. M. Hare, *Moral Thinking* (Oxford University Press, 1981)
Alex de Tocqueville, *Democracy in America* [1835–40]; trans. Henry Reeve (J Walker & Co., 1847)
John Rawls, *A Theory of Justice* (Harvard University Press, 1971)

Which of us should look after the baby?
Virginia Woolf, *A Room of One's Own* [1929] (Penguin Classics, 2002)
Aristotle, *Politics* [350 BCE]; trans. Benjamin Jowett (Clarendon Press, 1885)
Plato, *The Republic* [c. 380 BCE]; trans. Benjamin Jowett (Clarendon Press, 1888)
Mary Wollstonecraft, *A Vindication of the Rights of Women* (1792)
John Stuart Mill, *The Subjection of Women* (1869)
Germaine Greer, *The Female Eunuch* [1973] (Harper Perennial Modern Classics, 2006)
Simone de Beauvoir, *The Second Sex* [1949]; trans. H M Parshley (Penguin, 1972)
Kate Millet, *Sexual Politics* (Rupert Hart-Davis, 1970)
Laura Mulvey, "Visual Pleasure and Narrative Cinema", *Film Theory and Criticism: Introductory Readings*, ed. L Braudy and M Cohen (Oxford University Press, 1999)
Anita Sarkeesian, "Strategic Butt Coverings", www.Feminist Frequency.com (2016) https://feministfrequency.com/video/strategic-butt-coverings/ (accessed 15 September 2017)

I can't see the game as well as I'd like. Should I complain?
John Stuart Mill, *The Subjection of Women* (1869)
Carol Gilligan, *In A Different Voice* (Harvard University Press, 1982)
Harry Frankfurt, *The Importance of What We Care About* (Cambridge University Press, 1998)

Should my children benefit from my success?
Confucius, *Analects*, in *The Chinese Classics*, vol. 1; trans. James Legge (Trübner & Co., 1861)
John Stuart Mill, *Considerations on Representative Government* (1861)
Iris Marion Young, *Justice and the Politics of Difference* (Princeton University Press, 1990)
John Rawls, *A Theory of Justice* (Harvard University Press, 1971)

Do I earn enough?
John Rawls, *A Theory of Justice* (Harvard University Press, 1971)
Robert Nozick, *Anarchy, State and Utopia* (Basic Books, 1974)
G A Cohen, *Rescuing Justice and Equality* (Harvard University Press, 2008)
John Stuart Mill, *Principles of Political Economy* (1848)

Should the state recompense me for my bad luck?
Ronald Dworkin, *Sovereign Virtue* (Harvard University Press, 2000)
Elizabeth S. Anderson, "What is the Point of Equality?", *Ethics*, vol. 109, no. 2 (January 1999)

Chapter 3:

Do I have a duty to feed Hammy?
Thomas Hobbes, *Leviathan* (1651)
John Locke, *Second Treatise of Government* (1689)
John Locke, *United States Declaration of Independence* (1776)
David Hume, "Of the Original Contract", *Essays Moral, Political and Literary* (1748)
Jean-Jacques Rousseau, *The Social Contract* [1762]; trans. G D H Cole (J M Dent & Sons, 1923)

Should I leave the kids in charge when I go on holiday?
Max Stirner, *The Ego and Its Own* [1844]; trans. S T Byington (Benjamin R Tucker, 1907)
Thomas Hobbes, *Leviathan* (1651)
Peter Kropotkin, *Mutual Aid: A Factor of Evolution* (1902)

Should I put my life on the Internet?
Jeremy Bentham, "Panopticon", *Collected Works*, vol. 4 (William Tait, 1843)
Michel Foucault, *Discipline and Punish* (1975); trans. Alan Sheridan (Vintage, 1977)
Evgeny Morozov, *The Net Delusion* (Allen Lane, 2011)
Aldous Huxley, *Brave New World* (Chatto & Windus, 1932)
George Orwell, *Nineteen Eighty-Four* [1949] (Penguin Books, 1998)
Neil Postman, *Amusing Ourselves to Death* (Methuen, 1985)
Dave Eggers, *The Circle* (Alfred A Knopf, 2013)

Can I trust the news?
Neil Postman, *Amusing Ourselves to Death* (Methuen, 1985)
Protagoras, quoted in Plato, *Theaetetus*; trans. Benjamin Jowett (Oxford University Press, 1892)
Gorgias, entry in *Concise Routledge Encyclopedia of Philosophy* (Routledge, 2000)
Ellic Howe, *Nostradamus and the Nazis* (Aborfield, 1965)
Alison Flood, "'Post-truth' Named Word of the Year by Oxford Dictionaries", *The Guardian* (2016) https://www.theguardian.com/books/2016/nov/15/post-truth-named-word-of-the-year-by-oxford-dictionaries (accessed 15 September 2017)
Charles Arthur, "Facebook Emotion Study Breached Ethical Guidelines, Researchers Say", *The Guardian* (2014) https://www.theguardian.com/technology/2014/jun/30/facebook-emotion-study-breached-ethical-guidelines-researchers-say (accessed 15 September 2017)
Noam Chomsky and Edward S Herman, *Manufacturing Consent* (Vintage, 1988)

Bibliography

My teenage son calls me a "fascist" – am I?
Plato, *The Republic* [c. 380 BCE]; trans. Benjamin Jowett (Clarendon Press, 1888)
Karl Popper, *The Open Society and Its Enemies* [1945] (Routledge, 1994)
Hannah Arendt, *Origins of Totalitarianism* (Schocken Books, 1951)
Karl Marx, "The Victory of the Counter-Revolution in Vienna" [1848]; in *Marx & Engels Collected Works*, vol. 7 (Lawrence & Wishart, 1977)
Jean-Jacques Rousseau, *The Social Contract* [1762]; trans. G D H Cole (J M Dent & Sons, 1923)
Joseph Raz, *The Morality of Freedom* (Clarendon Press, 1986)

My new department miss their old boss. Should I just sack everyone?
Edmund Burke, *Reflections on the Revolution in France* (1790)
Niccolò Machiavelli, *The Prince* [1532]; trans. W K Marriott (J M Dent & Co., 1908)

Should I go to jail for some trees?
Henry David Thoreau, *Resistance to Civil Government* (1848)
Mohandas Gandhi, "Satyagraha Leaflet No. 13" (1919)
John Rawls, *A Theory of Justice* (Harvard University Press, 1971)
Banksy, *Cut It Out* (Weapons of Mass Disruption, 2004)
Sean Tejaratchi, "Death, Phones, Scissors", *Crap Hound* (1999)

Should I get married?
Aristotle, *Politics* [350 BCE]; trans. Benjamin Jowett (Clarendon Press, 1885)
St Thomas Aquinas, *Summa Theologica* (1225–74); trans. Fathers of the English Dominican Province (1947)
Jean-Jacques Rousseau, *Emile* [1762]; trans. Barbara Foxley (J M Dent & Sons, 1921)
Immanuel Kant, *Metaphysics of Morals* [1797]; trans. Mary J Gregor (Cambridge University Press, 1996)
Friedrich Engels, *The Origin of the Family, Private Property, and the State* (1884)
Sigmund Freud, *Civilisation and its Discontents* [1908]; trans. David McLintock (Penguin, 2002)

Chapter 4:

My plane has crashed on a desert island. How will I and the other surviving passengers get along until we are rescued?
John Locke, *An Essay Concerning Human Understanding* (1689)
Declaration of the Rights of Man and of the Citizen [1789], quoted in Peter McPhee, *Liberty or Death: The French Revolution* (Yale University Press, 2016)
United Nations, *Universal Declaration of Human Rights* (1948)
Plato, *The Republic* [c. 380 BCE]; trans. Benjamin Jowett (Clarendon Press, 1888)
H L A Hart, "Are There Any Natural Rights?", *Philosophical Review*, vol. 64, no. 2 (April 1955)

I've just seen a UFO! Why is the government lying to us?
Immanuel Kant, *Groundwork of the Metaphysic of Morals* [1785]; trans. H J Paton (Routledge, 1948)

Ronald Dworkin, *Taking Rights Seriously* (Harvard University Press, 1977)
Thomas Nagel, "Ruthlessness in Public Life", *Mortal Questions* (Cambridge University Press, 1979)

Should I emigrate to Mars?
Thomas Hobbes, *Leviathan* (1651)
John Locke, *Second Treatise on Government* (1689)
United Nations, *Universal Declaration of Human Rights* (1948)
Robert Nozick, *Anarchy, State and Utopia* (Basic Books, 1974)
Charles W Mills, *Black Rights, White Wrongs* (Oxford University Press, 2017)

Can I sack a robot?
Isaac Asimov, *Bicentennial Man* (Ballantine Books, 1976)
Nick Bostrom and Eliezer Yudkowsky, "The Ethics of Artificial Intelligence", *Cambridge Handbook of Artificial Intelligence*, ed. W Ramsey and K Frankish (Cambridge University Press, 2014)
John Searle, "Minds, Brains, and Programs", *Behavioral and Brain Sciences*, vol. 3, no.3 (February 1980)
Daniel Dennett, *Consciousness Explained* (Penguin, 1991)

Should my right to vote be based on my IQ?
Bryan Caplan, *The Myth of the Rational Voter* (Princeton University Press, 2007)
John Stuart Mill, *Considerations on Representative Government* (1861)
Peter Singer, *Practical Ethics* (Cambridge University Press, 1979)
René Descartes, *Discourse on Method* [1637]; trans. S Haldane and G R T Ross (Cambridge University Press, 1911)

There is a bomb somewhere. To what lengths should I go to find it?
United Nations, *Universal Declaration of Human Rights* (1948)
Stuart Hampshire, *Innocence and Experience* (Harvard University Press, 1989)
Niccolò Machiavelli, *The Prince* [1532]; trans. W K Marriott (J M Dent & Co., 1908)
Yuval Ginbar, *Why Not Torture Terrorists?* (Oxford University Press, 2008)

I am a teacher who's a part-time nude model – is that a problem?
Alison Lynch, "A Tale of Two Teachers: One is fired for modelling underwear; the other is given an Armani contract", *Metro* (2016) http://metro.co.uk/2016/03/28/a-tale-of-two-teachers-one-is-fired-for-modelling-underwear-the-other-is-given-an-armani-contract-5780292/ (accessed 15 September 2017)
Samuel Warren and Louis Brandeis, "The Right to Privacy", *Harvard Law Review*, vol. 4, no. 5 (December 1890)
William L. Prosser, "Privacy", *California Law Review*, vol. 48, no. 3 (1960)
Gabriel García Márquez, interview by Peter H. Stone, 'The Art of Fiction No. 69', *The Paris Review* 82 (1981).
Judith Jarvis Thomson, "The Right to Privacy", *Philosophy and Public Affairs*, vol. 4, no. 3 (July 1975)
Robert Bork, *The Tempting of America* (Free Press, 1990)
Louis D Brandeis, *Olmstead v. U.S.*, 277 U.S. 438 (1928) (dissenting)

Bibliography

My beliefs are in conflict with my job. What should I do?
John Locke, *Letter Concerning Toleration* (1689)
John Stuart Mill, *On Liberty* (1859)
Karl Popper, *The Logic of Scientific Discovery* [1934] (Routledge, 2002)
Thomas Kuhn, *The Structure of Scientific Revolutions* (University of Chicago Press, 1962)

Chapter 5:

Should I drink fair-trade coffee?
Marshall McLuhan, *The Gutenberg Galaxy* (University of Toronto Press, 1962)
Naomi Klein, *No Logo* (Harper Perennial, 2000)
Kieren McCarthy, "Another Death in Apple's 'Mordor' – its Foxconn Chinese assembly plant", www.theRegister.co.uk (2015) https://www.theregister.co.uk/2015/08/07/another_death_apple_assembly_plant/ (accessed 15 September 2017)
Kate Hodal, "Death Metal: Tin Mining in Indonesia", *The Guardian* (2012) https://www.theguardian.com/environment/2012/nov/23/tin-mining-indonesia-bangka (accessed 15 September 2017)
Bruce Wydick, "10 Reasons Fair-Trade Coffee Doesn't Work", *Huffington Post* (2016) http://www.huffingtonpost.com/bruce-wydick/10-reasons-fair-trade-coffee-doesnt-work_b_5651663.html? (accessed 15 September 2017)

Should I support my country going to war?
Marcus Tullius Cicero, *De Officiis* ("On Duty"); trans. Walter Miller (Heinemann, 1913)
St Augustine of Hippo, "Letter 189"; quoted in Aquinas, *Summa Theologica*
St Thomas Aquinas, *Summa Theologica*; trans. Fathers of the English Dominican Province (1947)
Sa'adi, *Bani Adam*, trans. M. Aryanpour, displayed at entrance to UN building in New York
The Holy Bible, King James Version, Cambridge Edition [1769]; www.KingJamesBibleOnline.org (2017)
Thomas Hobbes, *Leviathan* (1651)

It is rumoured that a hostile neighbouring state has developed nuclear weapons. Should I support my government in carrying out a pre-emptive strike?
Campaign for Nuclear Disarmament, "The Bombing of Hiroshima and Nagasaki", http://www.cnduk.org/campaigns/global-abolition/hiroshima-a-nagasaki (accessed 15 September 2017)
Atomic Archive, "The Atomic Bombings of Hiroshima and Nagasaki – Total Casualties" http://www.atomicarchive.com/Docs/MED/med_chp10.shtml (accessed 15 September 2017)
Atomic Heritage Foundation, "Tsar Bomba", (2014) http://www.atomicheritage.org/history/tsar-bomba (accessed 15 September 2017)
Alice Calaprice, *The New Quotable Einstein* (Princeton University Press, 2005)
William Poundstone, *Prisoner's Dilemma* (Anchor Books, 1992)

Should I support my country if it decides to intervene in another country's domestic affairs?
Gore Vidal, *The Decline and Fall of the American Empire* (Odonian Press, 1992)
Noam Chomsky, *Understanding Power* (Vintage, 2002)
George Orwell, *Nineteen Eighty-Four* [1949] (Penguin Books, 1998)
Zbigniew Brzezinski, *The Grand Chessboard* (Basic Books, 1997)
Amal Hamdan, "Afghanistan: The Soviet Union's Vietnam", www.AlJazeera.com (2003) http://www.aljazeera.com/archive/2003/04/2008410113842420760.html (accessed 15 September 2017)
John Stuart Mill, *On Liberty* (1859)
Vladimir Lenin, *Imperialism, the Highest Stage of Capitalism* [1917] (Resistance Books, 1999)
Naomi Klein, *The Shock Doctrine* (Knopf Canada, 2007)

A new political party promises "progressive change". Can I believe that it can offer anything new?
Francis Fukuyama, *The End of History and the Last Man* (Free Press, 1992)
John Gray, *Straw Dogs* (Granta, 2002)
John Gray, *Black Mass* (Penguin Books, 2007)

Should I have children?
United Nations, *World Population Prospects – 2017 Revision* (2017)
Thomas Robert Malthus, *Essay on the Principle of Population* (1798)
Derek Parfit, *Reasons and Persons* (Oxford University Press, (1984)

Should I give to charity?
Friedrich Hayek, *The Fatal Conceit* (Routledge, 1988)
Keane Bhatt, "Thomas Pogge on the Past, Present and Future of Global Poverty", www.Truth-Out.org (2011) http://www.truth-out.org/news/item/792:thomas-pogge-on-the-past-present-and-future-of-global-poverty (accessed 15 September 2017)
John Pilger, *The New Rulers of the World* (Verso, 2002)
Thomas W. Pogge, interview, "Thomas Pogge on the Past, Present and Future of Global Poverty", www.truth-out.org (2011) http://www.truth-out.org/news/item/792:thomas-pogge-on-the-past-present-and-future-of-global-poverty (accessed 15 September 2017)
Thomas W. Pogge, "Assisting the Global Poor" [2003], in *The Ethics of Assistance*, ed. D. K. Chatterjee (Cambridge University Press, 2004)
Peter Singer, "Famine, Affluence, and Morality", *Philosophy and Public Affairs*, vol. 1, no. 3 (Spring 1972)

Why does Hollywood think the future is so grim?
Thomas More, *Utopia* (1516)
Sir Francis Bacon, *New Atlantis* (1627)
Edward Bellamy, *Looking Backward: 2000 to 1887* (Ticknor & Co., 1888)
Ursula Le Guin, *The Dispossessed* (Harper & Row, 1974)
Rutger Bregman, *Utopia for Realists* (Bloomsbury, 2017)
Immanuel Kant, *Idea of a Universal History on a Cosmopolitical Plan* [1784]; trans. Thomas de Quincey, Collected Writings of Thomas de Quincey, vol. 9 (1890)

Index

Index

Index

Index

Acknowledgements

My gratitude must go to the following: Trevor Davies, Ella Parsons, Polly Poulter, Yasia Williams and everyone at Octopus, for their patience and hard work; Robert Anderson, for his wise pruning and helpful suggestions; Grace Helmer, for her wonderful illustrations, and saintly patience through countless revisions; Kerrie Grain, for ploughing through everything and being my philosophical sounding board; Professor Colin Bird, for his Rawlsian wisdom and generosity; to Eliot, for his Photoshop prowess, and also, along with the rest of my family, for putting up with my short-temper, griping, grumpiness and neglect (well, more so than usual).